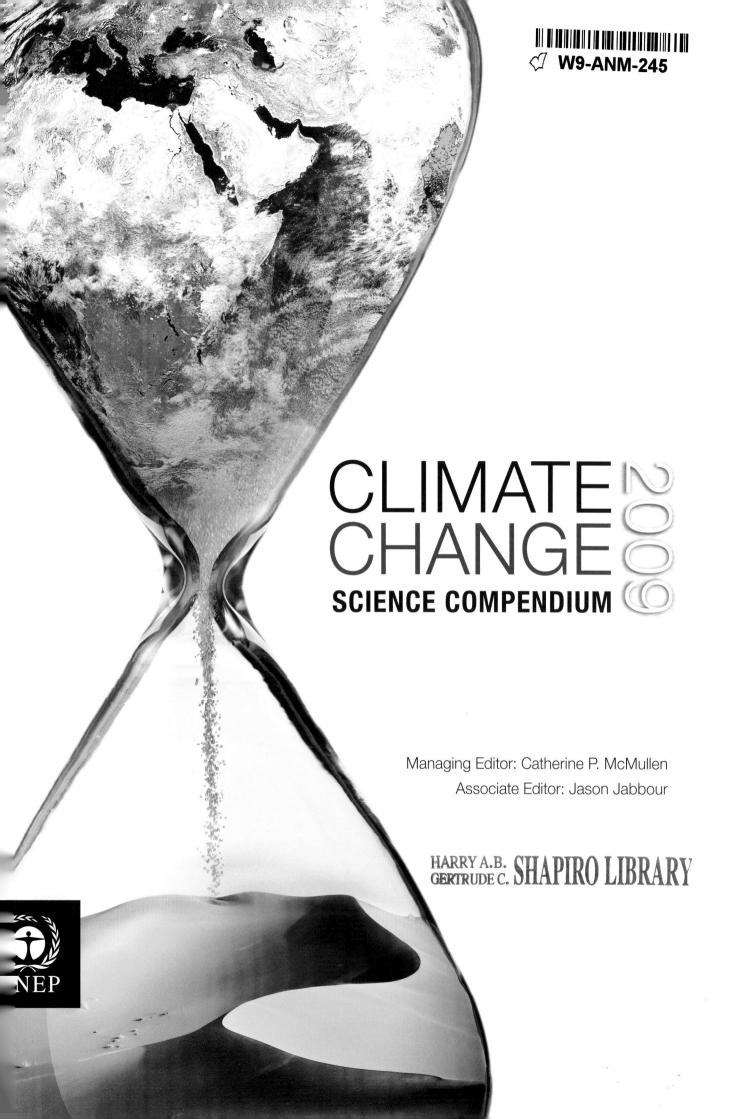

CLIMATE CHANGE 2009
SCIENCE COMPENDIUM

Managing Editor: Catherine P. McMullen

Associate Editor: Jason Jabbour

UNEP

Foreword

The science has become more irrevocable than ever: Climate change is happening. The evidence is all around us. And unless we act, we will see catastrophic consequences including rising sea levels, droughts and famine, and the loss of up to a third of the world's plant and animal species.

We need a new global agreement to tackle climate change, and this must be based on the soundest, most robust and up-to-date science available.

Through its overview of the latest definitive science, this Climate Change Science Compendium reaffirms the strong evidence outlined in the IPCC's 4th Assessment Report that climate change is continuing apace.

In fact, this report shows that climate change is accelerating at a much faster pace than was previously thought by scientists. New scientific evidence suggests important tipping points, leading to irreversible changes in major Earth systems and ecosystems, may already have been reached or even overtaken.

Climate change, more than any other challenge facing the world today, is a planetary crisis that will require strong, focused global action.

As pressures build for an internationally agreed response, we now have a once-in-a-generation opportunity to come together and address climate change through a newly invigorated multilateralism. This will be our chance to put in place a climate change agreement that all nations can embrace – an agreement that is equitable, balanced and comprehensive.

This Climate Change Science Compendium is a wake-up call. The time for hesitation is over. We need the world to realize, once and for all, that the time to act is now and we must work together to address this monumental challenge. This is the moral challenge of our generation.

Ban Ki-moon

Secretary-General of the United Nations
United Nations Headquarters, New York

September 2009

Preface

If governments are to make informed and transformative choices concerning climate change, they require the best and most up to date science.

Two years ago, in 2007, the Intergovernmental Panel on Climate Change's Fourth Assessment Report provided the world with conclusive proof that humans are altering the climate.

It also outlined a range of sobering impact scenarios covering sea-level rise and extreme weather events, as well as the implications for agricultural production, human health, and the marine food chain.

The IPCC's unique, consensus-led process has been at the centre of catalyzing a political response to the phenomena unfolding across the planet as a result of fossil fuel emissions and land use changes.

In a matter of a few weeks' time, governments will gather in Copenhagen, Denmark, for a crucial UN climate convention meeting. Many governments and stakeholders have requested an annual snapshot of how the science has been evolving since the publication of the IPCC's landmark fourth assessment in advance of the panel's next one in 2014.

This Climate Change Science Compendium, based on the wealth of peer-reviewed research published by researchers and institutions since 2006, has been compiled by UNEP in response to that request. The findings indicate that ever more rapid environmental change is underway with the pace and the scale of climate change accelerating, along with the confidence among researchers in their forecasts.

The Arctic, with implications for the globe, is emerging as an area of major concern. There is growing evidence that the ice there is melting far faster than had been previously supposed. Mountains glaciers also appear to be retreating faster. Scientists now suggest that the Arctic could be virtually ice free in September of 2037 and that a nearly ice-free September by 2028 is well within the realms of possibility. Recent findings also show that significant warming extends well beyond the Antarctic Peninsula to cover most of West Antarctica, an area of warming much larger than previously reported.

The impact on the Earth's multi-trillion dollar ecosystems is also a key area of concern. Under a high emission scenario—the one that most closely matches current trends—12–39 per cent of the planet's terrestrial surface could experience novel climate conditions and 10–48 per cent could suffer disappearing climates by 2100.

Rising levels of aridity are also concentrating scientific minds. New research indicates that by the end of the 21st century the Mediterranean region will also experience much more severe increases in aridity than previously estimated rendering the entire region, but particularly the southern Mediterranean, even more vulnerable to water stress and desertification.

While the Compendium presents current science, it can never replace the painstaking rigour of an IPCC process—a shining example of how the United Nations can provide a path to consensus among the sometimes differing views of more than 190 nations.

However, I hope the Compendium will provide important insights into the rapidly developing and fast moving realm of climate science so that the choices made by leaders in Copenhagen in December are informed by the best and the latest research available to the international community.

Achim Steiner

UN Under-Secretary General and Executive Director,
United Nations Environment Programme

September 2009

CONTENTS

EARTH SYSTEMS

Significant climate anomalies from 2007 to 200

Alaska (2007-2008) 2nd highest winter snowfall in 30 years.

Northern Hemisphere Snow Cover Extent (Jan 08) Largest January snow cover extent on record.

Arctic Sea-Ice (Sep 07) All-time lowest extent on record in September. Surpassed previous record set in 2005 by 23 per cent.

Arctic Sea-Ice (Oct 09) 2nd lowest extent on rec behind Sept 2007.

Central Canada (2008) Arctic air brought sub-zero temperatures. Lowest temperatures recorded: -36°C, with a wind chill of -50°C

United Kingdom (2008) One of 10 wettest summers on record.

US (2008) One of the top 10 years for tornado-related fatalities since 1953.

US (June 08) Heavy rain and worst floods since 1993 across the Midwest in June.

Canada (2008) Toronto's 3rd snowiest winter on record.

United Kingdom (2008-2009) Coldest winter since 1996/1997.

US (2008) 3rd worst fire season and persistent drought in western and southeastern US.

British Isles (Jan 09) Severe North Atlantic storm disrupted power to 100,000 homes across Ireland, and caused structural damage to buildings.

France and northe (Jan 09) We by storms 1 winds, equiva category 3 h

South California (Apr 09) Worst wildfire in 30 years scorched nearly 8,100 hectares in the area.

Tropical Storm Fay (Aug 08) 1st storm on record to strike Florida 4 times, max winds 100 km/hr.

Hurricane Bertha (Jul 08) Max winds - 205 km/hr. The longest-lived July Atlantic tropical storm on record (17 days).

Spain and Portugal (200 Worst drought for over a decade (Spain); worst winter since 1917 (Portu

Hurricane Norbert (Oct 08) Max winds - 220 km/hr. Most powerful 2008 East Pacific hurricane.

Hurricane Paloma (Nov 08) 2nd strongest November Atlantic hurricane on record. Max winds 230 km/hr.

Hurricane Omar (Oct 08) Max winds - 205 km/hr.

Northern Africa (Sep-Nov 08) Flooding affected tens of thous in Algeria and Morocco; worst floods in a century for Algeria.

Mexico (Aug 09) Worst drought in 70 years, affecting about 3.5 million farmers, with 80% of water reservoirs less than half full, 50,000 cows dead, and 17 million acres of cropland wiped out.

Hurricane Gustav (Aug 08) Worst storm to hit Cuba in 5 decades. Max winds 240 km/hr, with 341 km/hr wind in Paso Real San Diego, the highest in Cuba's history.

Hurricane Ike (Sep 08) Max winds 230 km/hr, 3rd most destructive US hurricane after Katrina.

Tropical Storm Alma (May 08) Max winds 105 km/hr; farthest east tropical storm to form in the eastern Pacific since 1970.

Northeastern Brazil (Apr 09) The worst deluge in more than 20 years in this normally semi-arid region, with floods and mudslides driving more than 186,000 people from their homes.

Ecuador (Feb 08) Heavy rain and worst flooding in the country's history.

Bolivia (Jan 08) Heavy rain and flooding.

Brazil (Nov 08) Heavy rain and flooding affected 1.5 million people.

Argentina, Paraguay, & Uruguay (Jan-Sep 08) Worst drought in over 50 years in some areas.

Chile (2008) Worst drought in 50 years in central and southern parts.

Source: NOAA 2007, NOAA 2008, NOAA 2009a

Fenno-Scandinavia (2008)
Warmest winter ever recorded in most parts of Norway, Sweden and Finland.

Northern Europe (Mar 08)
Powerful storms with wind gusts up to 160 km/hr.

ntral Europe (June 09). Flooding: rst natural disaster since 2002.

Middle East Region (Jan 08)
Heaviest snowfall in more than a decade in Iran. First snowfall in living memory in Baghdad, Iraq.

Iraq (July 09) Worst sandstorm in living memory, lasting more than a week.

Iraq (Aug 09) Experiences its 4th consecutive year of drought, with half the normal rainfall resulting in less than 60% of usual wheat harvest.

Eurasian Snow Cover Extent (Jan 08)
Largest January extent on record and smallest extent during March, April, and boreal spring.

Uzbekistan (Jan 08)
Coldwave with lowest temperatures in 40 years.

China (Jan 08) Worst severe winter weather in 5 decades affecting over 78 million people.

Tropical Cyclone Sidr (Nov 07) Max winds at landfall - 240 km/hr. The worst storm to hit Bangladesh since 1991. More than 8.5 million people affected and over 3,000 fatalities.

India (June 08) Heaviest rainfall in 7 years in Mumbai, Maharashtra.

India (June 09) Intense heat wave resulted in nearly 100 fatalities as temperatures soared past 40 °C.

China (Feb 09) Suffers worst drought in 50 years, threatening more than 10 million hectares of crops and affecting 4 million people.

Dhaka, Bangladesh (July 09) Received 11.4 inches of rain in the largest rainfall in a single day since 1949, leaving 12 million stranded.

Vietnam (Oct 08)
Heavy rain and floods.

Taiwan (Aug 09) Typhoon Morakot - worst flooding in 50 years with 83 inches of rain in southern parts.

Liaoning, China (Aug 09) Experienced worst drought in 60 years, affecting 5 million acres of arable land and more than 200,000 livestock.

Typhoon Hagupit (Sep 09)
Max winds 220 km/hr; worst typhoon to hit China's Guangdong province in more than a decade.

Philippines (Jan 09) Torrential downpours caused flash floods and landslides, forcing 200,000 to evacuate.

Tropical Cyclone Nargis (May 08)
Max winds 215 km/hr; most devastating cyclone in Asia since 1991.

Typhoon Neoguri (Apr 08)
Max winds 175 km/hr; earliest typhoon to strike China on record.

Eastern Philippine Islands (May 09) Typhoon Kujira triggered floods and major landslides, affecting over 246,000 people. Max winds were 213km/hr.

Typhoon Fengshen (Jun 08)
Max winds 205 km/hr. Philippines' worst maritime disaster since 1987.

Kenya (2009) Worst drought in almost two decades affecting 10 million people and causing crop failure.

heastern Africa (Jan 08)
ding in Mozambique, Malawi orst floods ever recorded nbabwe.

Tropical Cyclone Ivan (Feb 08)
Max winds 215 km/hr; one of the strongest cyclones ever in Madagascar.

South Africa (May-Jun 07)
Cold front led to 54 weather records in May. In June, Johannesburg received its 1st major snowfall since 1981.

Australia (Jan 09) Warmest January in the 1950-2008 record. Driest May on record. Drought conditions for over a decade in some parts.

Southern Australia, Adelaide (Jan 09)
On January 28, temperatures spiked to 45˚C; the hottest day in 70 years.

Southern Australia (2009)
Exceptional heat wave, triggering new temperature records and deadly wildfires, claims 210 lives.

New Zealand (2008)
Major winter cyclone caused flash floods and widespread wind damage across North Island in July.

Australia and New Zealand (2009)
Experienced their warmest August since records began 60 and 155 years ago, respectively.

Earth Systems

A thin veneer of atmosphere, soil, and water covers the surface of the planet. That is the envelope supplying most of the raw material we need to live. Energy from the Sun, with some residual energy still within the planet's core, feeds Earth's dynamic systems that cycle materials within the envelope. Earth System scientists are investigating the energy and material fluxes that determine the systems' dynamics to better understand climate change.

A thin veneer of atmosphere along the arc of the planet seen from a high altitude. *Source: A. Jordan, P. Cullis and E. Hall/NOAA*

INTRODUCTION

This Compendium presents some of the vanguard science and conceptual advances under discussion and published by researchers since 2006 that explores the challenge presented by climate change. Rapidly developing tools—that allow fast and accurate readings of environmental conditions, that compile and analyze data series of increasing complexities at unprecedented rates, and that allow insights into fluxes of energy and material at micro and macro scales—have accelerated the rate at which vanguard science is being produced.

In 1988, the World Meteorological Organization (WMO) and the United Nations Environment Programme (UNEP) established the Intergovernmental Panel on Climate Change (IPCC) as a scientific body to evaluate the risk of climate change and whether it could be caused by human activity.

Based on the findings of the first IPCC assessment, the United Nations Framework Convention on Climate Change (UNFCCC) was negotiated as an international environmental treaty produced at the United Nations Conference on Environment and Development in 1992. The treaty is aimed at stabilizing greenhouse gas concentrations in the atmosphere at a level that would prevent 'dangerous anthropogenic interference with the climate system'.

The IPCC produced its second, third, and fourth reports in 1995, 2001, and 2007 respectively, as well as a number of special reports on standardizing methodologies and focusing on particular concerns. The four IPCC Assessment Reports track scientists' growing understanding of Earth System complexities and present consensus conclusions of possible implications. The impressive body of analysis produced by collaboration among thousands of scientists and policy-makers is unrivalled and remains the final arbiter and consensus source of agreed scientific or political canon.

This Compendium serves a purpose different from the IPCC assessments. The questions addressed by the science presented here, simply concern where the frontiers of Earth System Science are evolving. What has been learned in the last few years? What is exciting the researchers and inspiring them to persist in their tests and experiments, their conceptual explorations? What is science telling us now about how climate is changing and why?

Background

Composed of different gases, the atmosphere circulates energy from the equator, where the Sun's radiation arrives most intensely, to the poles via weather systems such as cyclones, storms, and weather fronts. One of the most important circulation systems the atmosphere supports is the hydrologic cycle: Water evaporates from seas, lakes, rivers, soils, ice (sublimation), and plants (evapotranspiration) and moves through the atmosphere to precipitate as rain or snow—the precipitation that falls during monsoons and other events forms streams, rivers, lakes, permeating into soils and then into aquifers and groundwater. Plants send out roots to tap water and minerals in soils and use the Sun's energy to photosynthesize and grow. Snow solidifies into ice sheets and glaciers and in spring ice and snow melt to feed the streams and rivers that provide the water for forests and meadows and fields. Fresh water is delivered to oceans creating deltaic and coastal environments that support brackish water ecosystems such as tidal flats and mangrove forests.

Climate on Earth is affected by a myriad of drivers that operate over weeks and over geological eras. Long-term changes in average temperature and surface cover are dependent on orbital forcing, freshwater pulses, volcanic activity, variations in solar output, and the relative positions of continents and oceans, among other factors. Within the atmosphere, proportions of gases affect how much solar radiation reaches the Earth's surface to be absorbed and stored as heat. The composition of the atmosphere also affects how much of that heat, as longwave radiation from the Earth's surface, is then lost again into space, and how much is retained to circulate through Earth Systems.

Water vapour, which passes through the atmosphere in a matter of days or weeks, and other aerosols, can form clouds and affect radiation transfers in feedback systems. Aerosols have a strong influence on radiation fluxes,

Figure 1.1: The greenhouse effect

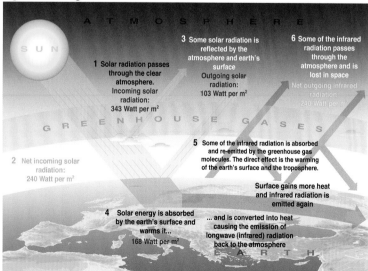

1 Solar radiation passes through the clear atmosphere. Incoming solar radiation: 343 Watt per m²

2 Net incoming solar radiation: 240 Watt per m²

3 Some solar radiation is reflected by the atmosphere and earth's surface. Outgoing solar radiation: 103 Watt per m²

4 Solar energy is absorbed by the earth's surface and warms it... 168 Watt per m²

... and is converted into heat causing the emission of longwave (infrared) radiation back to the atmosphere

5 Some of the infrared radiation is absorbed and re-emitted by the greenhouse gas molecules. The direct effect is the warming of the earth's surface and the troposphere. Surface gains more heat and infrared radiation is emitted again

6 Some of the infrared radiation passes through the atmosphere and is lost in space. Net outgoing infrared radiation: 240 Watt per m²

Solar radiation is absorbed by the Earth's surface, causing the Earth to warm and to emit infrared radiation. The greenhouse gases then trap the infrared radiation, warming the atmosphere. *Source: UNEP/GRID-Arendal 2002*

as they can either block or enhance delivery of shortwave radiation or escape of longwave radiation. Other components of the atmosphere can influence how much radiation reaches the Earth's surface and how much escapes. Those gases that remain in the atmosphere for decades and longer and that inhibit the escape of longwave radiation are called 'greenhouse gases' (GHGs).

One of the most common GHGs is carbon dioxide, an essential link between plants and animals. Animals produce carbon dioxide and exhale it, while plants absorb carbon dioxide during photosynthesis, store it within their material structures, and then release it when they respire. Plant material decomposes as bacteria and other organisms consume the mass, releasing more carbon dioxide back to the atmosphere. In the absence of oxygen, bacteria produce methane, the second most common GHG. Since the advent of the Industrial Revolution, in the mid 18th century, intense and inefficient burning of wood, charcoal, coal, oil, and gas, accompanied by massive land use change, has resulted in increased concentrations of GHGs in the Earth's atmosphere. The use of artificial fertilizers, made possible by techniques developed in the late 19th century, has led to practices resulting in releases of nitrous oxide, another GHG, into air. Since the 1920s, industrial activities have applied a number of manmade carbon compounds for refrigeration, fire suppression, and other purposes some of which have been found to be very powerful GHGs (UNEP 2009).

Climate and Earth Systems

In 1957 and 1958, the International Geophysical Year (IGY) produced a coordinated effort to fill gaps in scientific understanding of the Earth using innovative technologies such as rockets, radar, and computers (NOAA-ESRL 2008). Among the many observations and research programmes that originated from IGY, measurements of the gases that comprise the Earth's atmosphere—and the fluctuations in their proportions—provided new insights to the field of study that is now known as Earth System Science.

Measurements of carbon dioxide taken at the Mauna Loa Observatory in Hawaii revealed that the proportion of carbon dioxide in the atmosphere increases during the northern hemisphere autumn and winter and decreases in spring and summer. This cycle tracked the varying rates of plant photosynthesis during the year. The seasons of the northern hemisphere dominate this cycle because of the overwhelming amount of land in that hemisphere compared to the vast ocean coverage in the south. As observations continued for years and then decades, scientists realized that while the annual variations went up and down, the overall trend of carbon dioxide in the atmosphere was going up (Keeling and Whorf 2005).

Debates among scientists continued, as more and more data were collected and information was extracted from many of the programmes

Figure 1.2: Atmospheric CO$_2$: Mauna Loa measurements

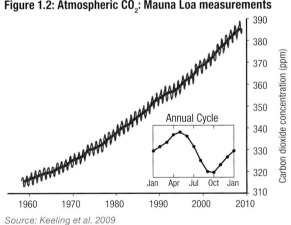

Source: Keeling et al. 2009

Figure 1.3: Surface temperature anomalies relative to 1951–1980 from surface air measurements at meteorological stations and ship and satellite SST measurements

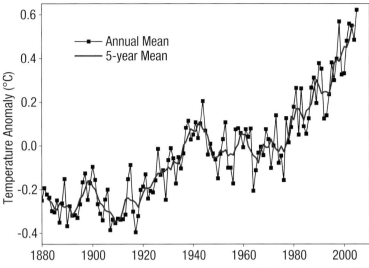

Source: Hansen et al. 2006

established in the Earth Sciences since IGY. Some of the most intriguing information described the fluctuations of ice sheets across the northern hemisphere for the previous 1.5 to 2.5 million years. Those fluctuations or pulses of ice coverage could last for hundreds of thousands of years, according to measurements of elemental isotope ratios of compounds trapped in coral reefs, ocean sediments, and ice cores. At the same time the atmospheric evidence of the ice pulses was being documented, examination of forcing from orbital variations suggested the Earth could be ending the interglacial period during which human civilization had flourished. But correlations between the trends of carbon dioxide in the atmosphere and the average global temperature appeared to be very strong: Over a 1000-year period, a fairly level trend seemed to start a sharp rise since the late 1800s. Was the climate changing—and, if so, how? And could human activity possibly have anything to do with

Box 1.1: Formalizing Earth System Science

In 2001, scientists from around the world gathered in Amsterdam to formally establish an interdisciplinary field of study called Earth System Science. The Amsterdam Declaration on Global Change defines the parameters:

1) The Earth System behaves as a single, self-regulating system comprised of physical, chemical, biological, and human components.

2) Human activities are significantly influencing Earth's environment in many ways in addition to greenhouse gas emissions and climate change.

3) Global change cannot be understood in terms of a simple cause-effect paradigm.

4) Earth System dynamics are characterized by critical thresholds and abrupt changes.

5) Human activities could inadvertently trigger such changes with severe consequences for Earth's environment and inhabitants.

6) In terms of some key environmental parameters, the Earth System has moved well outside the range of the natural variability exhibited over the last half million years at least.

7) An ethical framework for global stewardship and strategies for Earth System management are urgently needed.

Source: Earth System Science Partnership 2001

it? To answer such questions, researchers needed to use innovative approaches working with interdisciplinary teams that could incorporate data, information, and knowledge from many sources.

Demand for innovative approaches came from many directions, not the least from multinational environmental agreements. The UNFCCC's Article 2 commits signatory nations to stabilizing greenhouse gas concentrations at levels that prevent dangerous anthropogenic interference with the climate system. This stabilization is to be achieved within a timeframe that is sufficient to allow ecosystems to adapt naturally to climate change, to ensure that food production is not threatened, and to enable economic development to proceed in a sustainable manner. The debate about what is dangerous anthropogenic interference and what is a sufficient timeframe has continued since the convention came into force in 1994. The scientific interdisciplinary approach, that has developed to study the Earth as a dynamic meta-system, partly in response to these and other questions about Global Environmental Change, is Earth System Science.

HOW EARTH SYSTEM SCIENCE WORKS

Earth System scientists incorporate data from a global network of over 11,000 ground stations that provide daily records of temperatures, precipitation, barometric pressure, and atmospheric concentrations of various compounds into their analyses of how the Earth System works (WMO 2009). These are records of the Essential Climate Variables. Data and information also emerge from specifically defined research projects designed to answer questions about the nature and the rates of change in natural systems.

Interpretation of data from research projects, ground stations, ocean monitoring, and satellite observation systems is a critical contribution to our understanding of changes in the climate system and to the identification of the most effective and efficient response options to these changes (WMO 2009).

Recent scientific and technological developments allow for more accurate modelling of climate change and its impacts. At the same time, looking into the past and studying historical changes in climate can help us to make more sense of the present and to better predict the future.

Global observing systems

In the 1980s, several UN agencies recognized the need for a comprehensive, long-term, global monitoring programme to observe phenomena related to climate change. Today, three inter-related global observing systems to monitor the Earth's environment are organized by these UN agencies in cooperation with the scientific community and national governments.

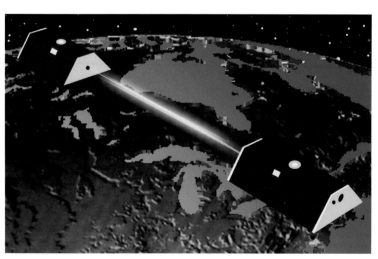

The twinned GRACE satellites bring new dimensions to Earth observations.
Source: NASA 2006a

The Global Climate Observing System aims to provide comprehensive information on the total climate system through the collection of data on long-term climate change. The Global Ocean Observing System implements observation programmes for the oceans and coastal areas, respective to five programme areas: Climate Change and Variability, Marine Living Resources, Oceanographic Data Services, the Coastal Zone, and Health of the Oceans (GCOS 2009). The Global Terrestrial Observing System develops and networks observations of longterm changes in land quality, availability of freshwater resources, pollution and toxicity, loss of biodiversity, and climate change (GTOS 2009). Together, these systems provide vital data on the Earth System and climate change.

Satellite capabilities

There are at least eight Earth observing satellite projects in operation that are formally part of the UN-managed programme. In addition, many nations operate weather satellites and commercial interests have also begun to contribute to the monitoring of the planet and its environment. The Gravity Recovery and Climate Experiment (GRACE) is one example of how advances in satellite technology are dramatically improving our understanding of Earth's natural systems and the ways in which they are changing. The GRACE project utilizes two identical spacecrafts flying in tandem approximately 220 kilometres apart in a polar orbit 500 kilometres above the Earth. As the twin satellites fly in formation over Earth, the speed of each and the distance between them are constantly communicated via a microwave interferometer ranging instrument (NASA JPL 2009). As the gravitational field below the satellites changes, correlating to changes in mass and topography, the orbital motion of each satellite is changed, and this is measured in response to variations in the pull of gravity. From this, the surface mass fluctuations in the Earth's gravitational field can be determined. The satellite pair completes a full Earth orbit every 30 days, allowing researchers to build a monthly picture of the Earth's gravitational field and to track variations and trends in gravitational fluxes of water and ice, as well as land mass.

The gravity variations that GRACE detects include those related to surface and deep currents in the ocean, runoff and groundwater storage in land masses, exchanges between ice sheets or glaciers and the oceans, and variations of mass within the Earth, such as those associated with tectonic and volcanic processes (Rodell *et al.* 2009). The combination of advanced gravity models with ocean height measurements from satellite altimeters and data from the GRACE satellites enables a far more detailed study of global ocean circulation than previously possible.

Ocean monitoring

Earth's oceans play an integral role in the global climate system. Regular scanning of the ocean surface is vital to building a database of ocean surface topography that can help predict short-term changes in weather and longer term patterns of climate. Historically, ships navigating the world's oceans have gathered observations of this nature, and so the resulting data has been restricted to main shipping routes.

Since 2000, the ship-based observations are being complemented by more precise information from an array of Argo ocean buoys, which provide accurate, reliable oceanographic data to monitor currents, the oceans' transport of heat and fresh water around the globe, and sea-level rise. The Argo system collects high-quality temperature and salinity profiles from the upper 2,000 metres of the ice-free global oceans—the layer that exchanges heat, chemicals, and moisture most readily with the terrestrial and atmospheric environments (NASA JPL 2009).

The battery-powered, autonomous floats are released to drift at a depth where they are stabilized by being neutrally buoyant. They are programmed to surface at typically ten-day intervals by pumping fluid into an external bladder and rising to the surface over a period of about six hours, measuring temperature and salinity along the way. These data are then transmitted from the surface to satellites, which also record the position of the buoys, before they deflate and sink to drift until the cycle is repeated (UCSD 2009).

The first Argo floats were deployed in 2000 and the array was complete in 2007, comprising over 3,300 floats to date. The array is made up of 23 different countries' contributions that range from a single float to much larger deployments (NASA JPL 2008). The Argo system has become a major component of the ocean observing system and is now the main source of data on subsurface temperature and salinity fluctuations in oceans—critically important factors in understanding global climate change.

Geological research

Paleoclimate research has both theoretical and applied scientific objectives. Evidence of past climates helps us to more fully understand the evolution of the Earth's atmosphere, oceans, biosphere, and cryosphere. At the same time, paleoclimate studies help us to quantify properties of Earth's climate, including the forces that drive climate change and the sensitivity of the Earth's climate to those forces. When scientists investigate causes or complex processes in the present and future, they may find evidence in the past that helps them in mapping out the complexities.

For instance, about 55 million years ago an event known as the Paleocene-Eocene Thermal Maximum occurred. This was an episode of rapid and intense warming lasting less than 100,000 years (Eldrett *et al.* 2009). Scientists have suggested that methane released by warming and rising sea levels on continental shelves may have contributed to this and other similar events displayed in the geologic record (Schmidt and Shindell 2003, Archer 2007). Another paleoclimatic analogue comes from the 1980s and 1990s research into freshwater pulses introduced to the North Atlantic between 8,000 and 15,000 years ago by the deteriorating Laurentide Ice Sheet—work that stimulated much of the basis for today's study of the formation of the North Atlantic Deepwater Conveyer (Broecker *et al.* 1989, Clark *et al.* 2002). These studies inform us about the possibilities and implications of feedbacks and thresholds that could be recreated under modern, anthropogenically initiated conditions.

Modelling

Models are fundamental tools for understanding climate variations, allowing the synthesis of relevant atmospheric, oceanographic, cryospheric and land-surface data, and providing predictions of natural and anthropogenic climate change. Models are tested by their success at 'hindcasting' the conditions revealed by paleoclimate studies. Once they have established their ability to accurately represent past conditions, models are then refined for projecting trends into the future.

In 2008, the World Climate Research Program and the World Weather Research Programme convened a group of experts to review the current state of modelling, and to suggest a strategy for "seamless" prediction of weather and climate, from days to centuries. A major conclusion of the group was that projections from the current generation of climate models were insufficient in providing accurate and reliable predictions of regional climate change, including the statistics of extreme events and high impact weather, which are required for regional and local adaptation strategies. A new modelling system has been designed that predicts both internal variability and externally forced changes, and forecasts surface temperature with substantially improved skill throughout a decade, globally and in many regions (WMO 2009).

Decadal prediction

A new field of study, 'decadal prediction', is emerging in Earth System Science. Decadal prediction focuses between seasonal or inter-annual forecasting and longer term climate change projections, and explores time-evolving, regional climate conditions over the next 10 to 30 years. Numerous assessments of climate information user needs have identified the importance of this timescale to infrastructure planners, water resource managers, and other stakeholders (Meehl *et al.* 2009).

Several methods have been proposed for initializing global coupled-climate models for decadal predictions, all of which involve global time-evolving and three-dimensional ocean data, including temperature and salinity. An experimental framework to address decadal predictions has been incorporated into the most recent phase of the ongoing coupled model intercomparison project, some of which will be assessed for the use in the IPCC Fifth Assessment Report (AR5). The experimental framework will

Table 1.1: Cause and relative magnitudes of the major anthropogenic and natural influences on the climate over the period 1750-2007

Influence on solar and/or infrared radiation	Primary source of the influence	Resulting climate forcing (W/m^2) from 1750 to 2000	Persistence of the influence after sources are reduced	Resulting climate forcing (W/m^2) update from IPCC AR4 (2007)
Increased presence of contrails and cirrus clouds	Mainly a result of water vapor emissions from aircraft	+0.02	Days	+0.02
Increase in the concentrations of black soot and other aerosols	Emissions from fossil fuel combustion and biomass burning	+0.4	Days to weeks	+0.4
Increase in the loading of sulphate and other reflective aerosols	Mainly a result of coal combustion	-0.9	Days to weeks	-0.5
Cloud-forming effects of an increased loading of atmospheric particles	Mainly due to emissions from fossil fuel combustion and biomass burning	-0.7	Days to weeks	-0.7
Increased concentrations of mineral dust aerosols	Mainly from wind lofting from cleared areas of land	-0.6 to +0.4	Days to weeks	-0.6 to +0.4
Increase in the atmospheric CH_4 concentration	Emissions from rice agriculture, ruminants, energy production, biomass burning, and landfills	+0.5	Decades	+0.07
Decrease in the concentrations of stratospheric ozone	Mainly from chemical reactions caused by halocarbon emissions, aggravated by stratospheric cooling caused by increasing atmospheric concentrations of greenhouse gases	-0.15	Decades	-0.05
Increased surface reflectivity	Mainly a result of clearing vegetation from land areas	-0.2	Decades to centuries	-0.2
Increase in the atmospheric N_2O concentration	Emissions from agriculture cattle and feedlots, industry, and biomass burning	+0.15	Centuries	+0.15
Increase in the atmospheric CO_2 concentration	Emissions from fossil fuel combustion, deforestation, etc.	+1.5	Centuries and longer	+1.66
Increase in the concentrations of atmospheric halocarbons	Emissions from refrigeration, foam, industry, fire protection, and agriculture	+0.3	Centuries and longer, even out to millennia	+0.3
Total of human-induced factors (using central estimates)		**~+1.2**		**~+1.6**
Natural influences on radiative forcing				
Solar radiation incident at the top of atmosphere	Natural variation in solar intensity, with possible cycles from 11 years to several centuries, and changes in the Earth's orbital parameters over tens of thousands of years	+0.3 increase since lower-than-average value in 1750	A few years	+0.12 Increase since lower-than-average value in 1750
Decrease in solar radiation reaching the lower atmosphere due to volcanic eruptions	Natural event, occuring intermittently	near 0 (typical range is from about 0 to -4)	A few years to decades	near 0 (typical range is from about 0 to -4)

Source: Adapted from SEG 2007, Solomon et al. 2007, Metz et al. 2007

Figure 1.4: Fossil fuel emissions: Actual vs IPCC scenarios

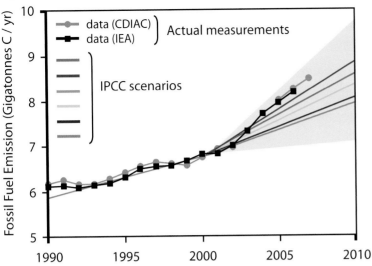

Anthropogenic emissions from fossil fuels increased by 38 per cent from the reference year 1990. The growth rate of emissions was 3.5 per cent per year for the period 2000-2007, an almost four-fold increase from 0.9 per cent per year in 1990-1999. The actual emissions growth rate for 2000-2007 exceeded the highest forecast growth rates for the decade 2000-2010 in the emissions scenarios of the IPCC Special Report on Emissions Scenarios (SRES). This makes current trends in emissions higher than the worst case IPCC-SRES scenario. The shaded area indicates the uncertainties around the projections. *Source: Raupach et al. 2007*

likely guide this emerging field over the next five years (WMO 2009, Meehl *et al.* 2009).

These are the main tools at scientists' disposal for monitoring, analyzing, and understanding the immense complexities of Earth Systems. Modern information and communication technologies have revolutionized modern science within the last two decades.

READING THE SIGNS

As we have seen, these new dimensions of understanding have revealed disturbing trends. Earth System scientists are becoming more concerned about dangerous anthropogenic interference and concepts like irreversibility. They are using the term 'committed' to define the natural responses of the Earth's systems to the increased GHG concentrations in the atmosphere and to the resulting increase in radiative forcing that brings higher global mean temperatures. Manifestations of these responses may be delayed, but once initiated they are all too likely irreversible.

» Already we are committed to ocean acidification that will damage or destroy coral reefs and the many species of marine life that inhabit or depend upon the ecosystem services of the reefs.

» Already we are committed to sea-level rise (SLR) over the next millennium.

» Already we are committed to tropical and temperate mountain glacier loss that will disrupt irrigation systems and hydroelectric installations, as well as alter the socio-economic and cultural lives of perhaps 20-25 per cent of the human population.

» Already we are committed to shifts in the hydrologic cycle that may result in the disappearance of regional climates with associated ecosystem disruption and species extinction as drylands shift poleward with the expansion of the intertropical convergence zone and bordering subtropical climates.

Projections of these consequences from increased GHG concentrations in the atmosphere extend over this century and through this millennium. The century timeframe affects many of those alive today—and certainly their children and grandchildren. The millennium timescale affects the development of our civilization: We still utilize canals, roads, and irrigation systems that were planned and constructed more than two millennia ago, and we still farm lands that were claimed from the ocean a thousand years ago. When we talk about a millennium we are talking about the civilization we have built (Lenton *et al.* 2008).

However, the projections and scenarios that define these unavoidable results may in some cases underestimate the actual impacts (Smith *et al.* 2009). Created in the 1990s, these scenarios all assumed that political will or other phenomena would have brought about the reduction in GHG emissions by this point in the 21st century.

In fact, CO_2 emissions from fossil-fuel burning and industrial processes have been accelerating at a global scale, with their growth rate increasing from 1.1 per cent per year for 1990–1999 to 3.5 per cent per year for 2000–2007. The emissions growth rate since 2000 was greater than for the most fossil-fuel intensive of the Intergovernmental Panel on Climate Change emissions scenarios developed in the late 1990s. Global emissions growth since 2000 has been driven by growing populations and per capita gross domestic product. Nearly constant or slightly increasing trends in the carbon intensity of energy have been recently observed in both developed and developing regions due to increasing reliance on coal. No region is substantially decarbonizing its energy supply. The emission growth rates are highest in rapidly developing economies, particularly China. Together, the developing and least-developed economies—80 per cent of the world's population—accounted for 73 per cent of the global growth in 2004 emissions, but only 41 per cent of total global emissions and only 23 per cent of cumulative emissions since 1750 (Raupach *et al.* 2007, Canadell and Raupach 2009).

Implications

Concentrations of atmospheric CO_2 are increasing rapidly because of two processes. Firstly, the growth of the world economy in the early 2000s, combined with an increase in its carbon intensity, has led to rapid growth in fossil fuel CO_2 emissions. Comparing the 1990s with 2000–2006, the emissions growth rate increased from 1.3 per cent to 3.3 per cent per year. The second process is indicated by increasing evidence of a decline in the efficiency of CO_2 sinks in oceans and on land in absorbing anthropogenic emissions. The decline in sink efficiency is consistent with results of climate–carbon cycle models, but the magnitude of the observed signal appears larger than that estimated by the models. All of these changes characterize a carbon cycle that is generating stronger-than-expected and sooner-than-expected climate forcing (Canadell *et al.* 2007, Le Quéré *et al.* 2007).

The climate forcing arriving sooner-than-expected includes faster sea-level rise, ocean acidification, melting of Arctic sea-ice cover, warming of polar land masses, freshening in ocean currents, and shifts in circulation patterns in the atmosphere and the oceans (Rahmstorf *et al.* 2009, Guinotte *et al.* 2008, Stroeve *et al.* 2008, McPhee *et al.* 2009, Seidel *et al.* 2008, MacDonald *et al.* 2008, Böning *et al.* 2008, Oldenborgh *et al.* 2008, Karl *et al.* 2009).

Scientific findings point to the possibility of abrupt changes in the Earth System (Zachos *et al.* 1993, Manabe and Stouffer 1995, Severinghaus *et al.* 1998, Severinghaus and Brook 1999, Clark *et al.* 2002, Alley *et al.* 2003, Clark and Weaver 2008, Severinghaus *et al.* 2009, Weaver *et al.* 2008). Acceptance of such a possibility has led to a number of studies that consider the behaviour of Earth Systems within that context. Resisting consideration of 'catastrophic' events to explain physical evidence is a residual effect from the false dichotomy in early Earth Science that resulted in catastrophist vs. uniformitarian contention in the 19th and earlier 20th centuries (Baker 1998). Today, abrupt change, thresholds, and irreversibility have come to the forefront in many analyses that have been published since 2007, reflecting research findings from the last three decades.

In early 2008, a team of scientists published the first detailed investigation of vulnerable Earth System components that could contain tipping points. The team used the term 'tipping element' for these vulnerable systems and accepted a definition for 'tipping point' as "...a critical threshold at which a tiny perturbation can qualitatively alter the state or development of a system..." (Lenton *et al*. 2008). They examined nine of these elements and assigned transition times to emphasize policy relevance. They also suggested the average global temperature increase that approaches a critical value within each tipping element. The study warned against a false sense of security delivered by projections of smooth transitions of climate change. Instead, too many critical thresholds could be crossed within the 21st century because of the changing climate.

Box 1.2: Tipping elements

There are nine tipping elements considered as Earth System components vulnerable to possible abrupt change. The time frames and threshold temperature increases presented here will likely be modified as new data and information track characteristics and rates of change:

Indian summer monsoon—The regional atmospheric brown cloud is one of the many climate change-related factors that could disrupt the monsoon. Possible time-frame: one year; temperature increase: unknown.

Sahara and West African monsoon—Small changes to the monsoon have triggered abrupt wetting and drying of the Sahara in the past. Some models suggest an abrupt return to wet times. Possible time-frame: 10 years; temperature increase: 3-5°C.

Arctic summer sea-ice—As sea-ice melts, it exposes darker ocean, which absorbs more heat than ice does, causing further warming. Possible time-frame: 10 years; temperature increase: 0.2-2°C.

Amazon rainforest—Losing critical mass of the rainforest is likely to reduce internal hydrological cycling, triggering further dieback. Possible time-frame: 50 years; temperature increase: 3-4°C.

Boreal forests—Longer growing seasons and dry periods increase vulnerability to fires and pests. Possible time-frame: 50 years; temperature increase: 3-5°C.

Atlantic Ocean thermohaline circulation—Regional ice melt will freshen North Atlantic water. This could shut down the ocean circulation system, including the Gulf Stream, which is driven by the sinking of dense saline water in this region. Possible time-frame: 100 years; temperature increase: 3-5°C.

El Niño Southern Oscillation (ENSO)—El Niño already switches on and off regularly. Climate change models suggest ENSO will enter a near-permanent switch-on. Possible time-frame: 100 years; temperature increase: 3-6°C.

Greenland Ice Sheet—As ice melts, the height of surface ice decreases, so the surface is exposed to warmer temperatures at lower altitudes which accelerates melting that could lead to ice-sheet break up. Possible time-frame: 300 years; temperature increase: 1-2°C.

West Antarctic Ice Sheet—The ice sheets are frozen to submarine mountains, so there is high potential for sudden release and collapse as oceans warm. Possible time-frame: 300 years; temperature increase: 3-5°C.

Source: Lenton et al. 2008

Scientists hope to establish early warning systems to detect when possible tipping elements become unstable. Detection of 'slowing down' of established variability before abrupt climate changes of the past offers a possible clue about tipping elements, thresholds (Dakos *et al*. 2008). The goal of early warning may be complicated by the cumulative effects the different Earth Systems have on each other, given the complex interactions among tipping elements at multiple scales and under various circumstances.

Conceptually, thresholds and tipping elements can be grasped, but the time-frames of the effects and the irreversibility of crossing such margins remain uncertain and need to be considered carefully. With the help of models, scientists have begun to estimate the conditions under which irreversible thresholds in the Earth System might be exceeded.

For example, focusing on two potentially irreversible consequences in Earth Systems, dry-season rainfall reductions in some regions and ongoing sea-level rise, researchers used models to look at the systems' response to increases in atmospheric CO_2 concentrations (Solomon *et al*. 2009). Based on an assumption that CO_2 will peak between 450 and 600 parts per million (ppm) in the next century, they project a 10 per cent increase in aridity, dominating the dry seasons in southern Africa, eastern South America, and southwestern North America. An increase in dry season aridity approaching 20 per cent would dominate in western Australia, northern Africa, and southern Europe. All these regions would experience wet-season precipitation somewhat lower or similar to current conditions, while southeast Asia would experience up to 5 per cent wetter rainy seasons and 10 per cent more arid dry seasons.

The model experiments show that a climate scenario in which CO_2 concentrations exceed 600 ppm in the 21st century might lead to a rise in the global average sea level of at least 0.4 to 1.0 metres, whereas a scenario with a peak concentration of 1000 ppm causes a sea-level rise of around 1.9 metres (Solomon *et al*. 2009). These figures only account for the thermal expansion of the sea. In these projections, a complete loss of glaciers and small ice caps within the next five centuries would add 0.2-0.7 metres to sea levels. While the researchers did not calculate contributions from the West Antarctic, East Antarctic, or Greenland Ice Sheets, they do suggest that even a partial loss from those ice sheets could 'add several meters or more to these values' (Solomon *et al*. 2009).

REASONS FOR CONCERN

In the IPCC's Third Assessment Report (TAR) scientists created an image to represent the possible risks associated with increases in global mean temperature (GMT) and explained particular reasons for concern. An updated image was not presented in the AR4 Synthesis Report, but the researchers who updated it published their findings in peer-reviewed literature (Smith *et al*. 2009).

The five reasons for concern cover risks to unique and threatened systems, risk of extreme weather events, distribution of impacts, aggregate damages, and the risks of large-scale discontinuities. The basis for choosing these reasons for concern are the magnitude, the timing, the persistence and reversibility, the distribution, and the likelihood of the impacts, as well as the potential for adaptation. The reasons for concern are analysed over temperature increases ranging from 0-5 degrees Celsius and assigned values represented by the intensity of colours running from white as no threat or risk, to yellow as some to moderate risk, and finally to deep red as high risk or very negative effects. In their 2008 update, the authors re-examined each of the reasons for concern and re-assigned colours and intensity from the additional information, as appropriate.

The shifting of risk transitions from 2000 to 2008 is based on an assessment of strengthened observations of impacts already occurring

Figure 1.5: Burning embers: Updated reasons for concern

TAR (2001) Reasons For Concern — **Updated Reasons For Concern**

Risks to Many | Large Increase | Negative for Most Regions | Net Negative in All Metrics | Higher

Negative for Some Regions; Positive for Others | Positive or Negative Market Impacts; Majority of People Adversely Affected | Very Low

Risks to Some | Increase

Risks to Unique and Threatened Systems | Risk of Extreme Weather Events | Distribution of Impacts | Aggregate Impacts | Risks of Large Scale Discontinuities

Risks to Many | Large Increase | Negative for Most Regions | Net Negative in All Metrics | High

Negative for Some Regions; Positive for Others | Positive or Negative Market Impacts; Majority of People Adversely Affected | Low

Risks to Some | Increase

Risks to Unique and Threatened Systems | Risk of Extreme Weather Events | Distribution of Impacts | Aggregate Impacts | Risks of Large Scale Discontinuities

Increase in Global Mean Temperature above circa 1990 (°C)

Future / Past

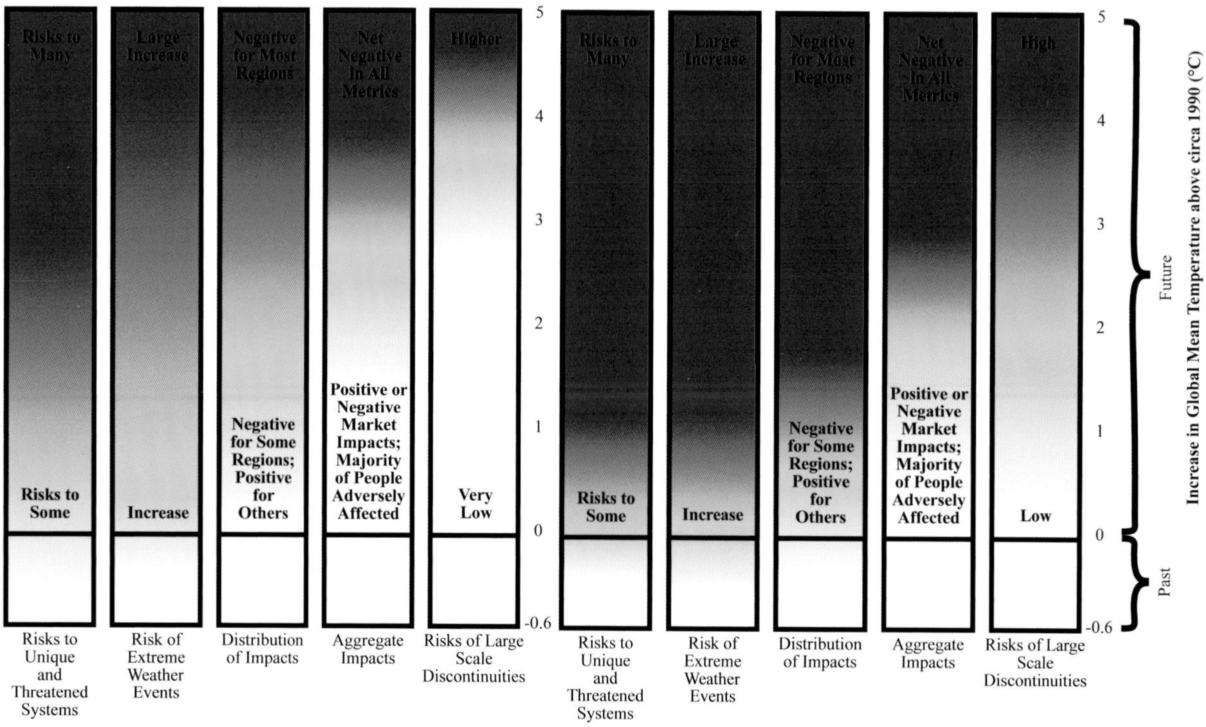

Climate change consequences are plotted against increases in degrees Celsius global mean temperature after 1990. Each column corresponds to a specific reason for concern and represents additional outcomes associated with increasing global mean temperature. *Source: Smith et al. 2009*

because of warming to date; better understanding and greater confidence in the likelihood of climatic events and the magnitude of impacts and risks associated with increases in GMT; more precise identification of particularly affected sectors, groups, and regions; and growing evidence that even modest increases in GMT above 1990 levels could commit the climate system to the risk of very large impacts over many centuries or even millennia.

Smaller increases in GMT are now estimated to lead to significant or substantial consequences in the framework of the five reasons for concern. The transitions from moderately significant risks to substantial or severe

Figure 1.6: Probability distribution for the committed warming by GHGs between 1750 and 2005. Shown are climate tipping elements and the temperature threshold range

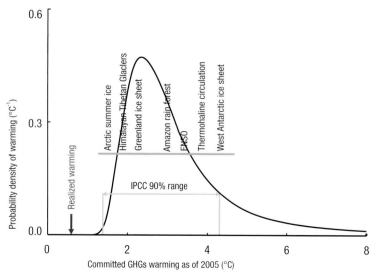

Source: Ramanathan and Feng 2008

risks for all of the concerns are at lower GMT increases above 1990 compared with the location of the transitions in the TAR.

In addition, for distribution of impacts, aggregate impacts, and large-scale discontinuities, the transition from no or little risk to moderately significant risk occurs at a smaller increase in GMT. The transition from no or little risk to moderately significant risk in the unique and threatened systems and extreme events concerns occurs at a lower increase in GMT because there are more and stronger observations of climate change impacts. The temperature range of moderately significant risks to substantial or severe risks for large-scale discontinuities is now much wider than the 2001 estimates in the TAR. In general, the figure illustrates that the temperatures risking 'dangerous anthropogenic interference' are very much within range (Smith *et al.* 2009).

The problem of avoiding the climate change thresholds before us calls for innovative and perhaps even unorthodox approaches, incorporating concepts such as tipping elements and cumulative effects in our risk assessments. As well, minimizing the importance of what we cannot quantify while focusing on parameters that are already well constrained should be avoided. Development of tools to help us comprehend the scale and duration of the climate changes we face, and the commiments we have already made, can only help in adopting optimal management strategies.

One of the most difficult additional factors to include accurately in estimates of radiative forcing at global, regional, and local scales are the effects of aerosols—particles that absorb solar radiation and particles that reflect solar radiation. To complicate matters, the same size particles may do either at different heights within the atmosphere. Aerosol particles come from dust picked up by wind and from a myriad of anthropogenic sources produced when people burn fuel, use diesel engines, and clear forests. The aerosols that reflect radiation are more common than those that absorb and they serve as a mask that prevents the full effect of GHG radiative forcing to heat the Earth. These aerosols form atmospheric brown clouds at height and cause health problems from their pollution at the Earth's surface. As they are addressed because of concerns about ground-level pollution, their climate change masking function will dwindle and temperatures will increase (Seinfeld 2008, Ramanathan and Carmichael 2008, Cox *et al.* 2008, Shindell and Faluvegi 2009, Hill *et al.* 2009, Paytan *et al.* 2009).

With estimates of 1-5 degrees Celsius as the range of GMT increase over 1750 levels as the threshold for tipping elements, and 0-5 degrees Celsius over 1990 levels as reasons for concern (Figure 1.5), some researchers are realizing that we have already committed ourselves to significant environmental changes (Lenton *et al.* 2008, Smith *et al.* 2009, Ramanathan and Feng 2008). The observed increase in GHG concentration since 1750 has most likely committed the world to a warming of 1.4-4.3 degrees Celsius above pre-industrial surface temperatures. According to one study, the equilibrium warming above pre-industrial temperatures that the world will observe is 2.4 degrees Celsius—even if GHG concentrations had been fixed at their 2005 concentration levels and without any other anthropogenic forcing such as the cooling effect of aerosols. The range of 1.4 to 4.3 degrees Celsius in the committed warming overlaps and surpasses the currently perceived threshold range of 1-3 degrees Celsius for dangerous anthropogenic interference with many of the same climate-tipping elements such as the summer Arctic sea-ice, Himalayan glaciers, and the Greenland Ice Sheet (Ramanathan and Feng 2008).

Researchers suggest that 0.6 degrees Celsius of the warming we committed to before 2005 has been realized so far. Most of the rest of the 1.6 degrees Celsius total we have committed to will develop in the next 50 years and on through the 21st century. The accompanying sea-level rise can continue for more than several centuries. Lastly, even the most aggressive CO_2 mitigation steps as envisioned now can only limit further additions to the committed warming, but not reduce the already committed GHGs warming of 2.4 degrees Celsius (Ramanathan and Feng 2008).

As outlined in Systems Management (Chapter Five), some positive ideas are emerging. However, they require immediate decisions that could take effect within the next few years (Ramanathan and Feng 2008, Schellnhuber 2008, Mignon *et al.* 2008, Moore and MacCracken 2009, Elzen and Höhne 2008, Meinshausen *et al.* 2009, Vaughan *et al.* 2009). These approaches and schemes require decisions about differentiated responsibilities and technology transfers. They require leadership and cooperation; tolerance, transparency, and honesty.

Perhaps experiences in everyday life have led us to believe that slow processes such as climate changes pose small risks, on the assumption that a choice can always be made to quickly reduce emissions and reverse any harm within a few years or decades.

This assumption is incorrect for carbon dioxide emissions due to the longevity of their effects in the atmosphere and because of ocean warming (Lenton *et al.* 2008, Solomon *et al.* 2009). Irreversible climate changes due to carbon dioxide emissions have already taken place. Continuing carbon dioxide emissions in the future means further irreversible effects on the planet, with attendant long legacies for choices made by contemporary society (Ramanathan and Feng 2008, Eby *et al.* 2009).

Applying discount rates to future costs with the assumption that more efficient climate mitigation can occur in a future world that is wealthier than ours ignores the irreversibility of the effects as well as the devastating consequences they will have on the wealth of future generations. We have already committed our civilization to considerable deficiencies in the integrity of Earth Systems. These dangers pose substantial challenges to humanity and nature, with a magnitude that is directly linked to the management practices we choose to retreat from further tipping points and irreversible changes from GHG emissions (Lenton *et al.* 2008, Solomon *et al.* 2009).

Where the river meets the sea on the Corcovado Pacific Coast, Costa Rica, creating one of many estuaries. These important estuary ecosystems create a rich and dynamic system that filters water, nurtures marine life, and provides coastal protection. *Source: Biosphoto/Michel & Christine Denis-Huot*

EARTH'S ICE

Earth's Ice

Accelerated shrinking of mountain glaciers on every continent, rapid reduction of Arctic sea-ice, disintegration of floating ice shelves, and increased melt rates of Earth's three Ice Sheets—Greenland, West Antarctic, and East Antarctic—provide compelling evidence of our changing climate.

Melting icebergs.
Source: Shutterstock

Ice on the Earth's surface makes up more than twice the volume of all other freshwater storage types including groundwater, lakes, and rivers. Significantly, this ice also contains almost 80 per cent of all the fresh water on the planet. As a central component of the Earth's climate system, ice is connected to interactions and feedbacks at global scales, including the planetary energy balance, sea-level change, and ocean circulation (UNEP 2007).

The Earth's surface ice on land can be divided into two categories, excluding seasonal snow: These are the three large ice sheets of Greenland, West Antarctica, and East Antarctica and the aggregate of all other glaciers and ice caps, including those surrounding the ice sheets but not connected to them. The Greenland and Antarctica Ice Sheets are by far the largest category, containing 12 per cent and 87 per cent of land ice volume, respectively. Glaciers and ice caps contain only about 1 per cent of global land ice volume. In sea level equivalent terms, if completely melted, Antarctica, Greenland, and the category of glaciers and ice caps would raise sea level by approximately 57 metres, 8 metres, and 0.7 metres, respectively. However, while the glaciers and ice caps are a very small source of potential sea-level rise, their rate of contribution to sea level currently exceeds the rates of both Antarctica and Greenland. The volume of glaciers and ice caps is poorly constrained by observations, with a range of estimates of total volume varying by more than a factor of five (Meier *et al.* 2007, Pfeffer *et al.* 2008).

GLACIERS AND ICE CAPS

Many glaciers and ice caps in polar, temperate, and high altitude tropical regions are experiencing retreat and volume loss. Diminishing glacier and ice cap volumes not only dominate current sea-level rise but also threaten

Solheimajokull outlet glacier, south Iceland. *Source: Oddur Sigurosson*

the well-being of approximately one-sixth of the world's population who depend on glacier ice and seasonal snow for their water resources during dry seasons (WGMS 2008b).

Documentation of this trend has been building for the last century and studies of glaciers and ice caps are becoming more sophisticated with new satellite-based observation technologies and attempts to distinguish glacier responses to multiple variables (WGMS 2008a, WGMS 2008b, Braithwaite 2009). Evidence from increasing loss rates is becoming stronger. In the European Alps, for instance, overall glacial volume reduced by about one per cent per year from 1975 to 2000 and between two and three per cent since the turn of the millennium (Haeberli *et al.* 2007).

Data from the World Glacier Monitoring Service track 30 reference glaciers in nine mountain ranges and document strongly accelerating loss of glacier mass. Since the year 2000, the mean loss rate of these 30 reference glaciers has increased to about twice the loss rates observed during the two decades between 1980 and 1999 (Zemp *et al.* 2009). The previous record loss in 1998 has been exceeded already three times—in 2003, 2004 and 2006—and the new record loss in 2006 is almost double that of the previous record loss in 1998. The mean annual loss for the decade 1996-2005 is more than twice the value measured between 1986 and 1995 and more than four times that of the period 1976-1985. Certain regions such as southern Alaska suffer from significantly higher losses (Larsen *et al.* 2007). Positive feedback mechanisms such as albedo change due to dark dust and collapse around glacier peripheries now appear to play an increasingly important role, enhancing mass loss beyond pure climate forcing (WGMS 2008a, WGMS 2008b, Oerlemans *et al.* 2009).

Among those glaciers losing the most volume in the record year of 2006, Norway's Breidalblikkbrae thinned by more than 3 metres in the year, France's Ossoue glacier thinned by almost 3 metres, and Spain's Maladeta glacier thinned by nearly 2 metres, thereby losing a considerable percentage of their remaining average ice thickness. Of the 30 reference glaciers, only one thickened in this extraordinary year, Echaurren Norte in Chile. The current extent and volume of glaciers and ice caps in many mountain ranges is now close to—or exceeding—the lowest value since the onset of the Holocene about 10,000 years ago (Solomina *et al.* 2008).

Figure 2.1: Mean cumulative specific mass balance of indicated glaciers

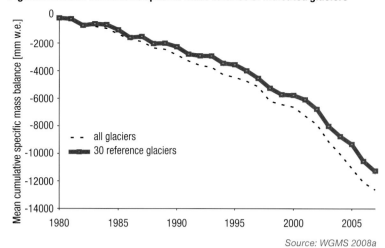

Source: WGMS 2008a

Glaciers and ice caps have a potentially significant but very poorly known dynamic response component because of the number of marine-terminating outlet glaciers draining them. In the Russian Arctic for example, iceberg calving accounted for about 30 per cent of observed volume loss during the period 1951-2001 (Glazovsky and Macheret 2006). At Austfona Ice Cap on Svalbard, calving accounts for approximately 35 per cent of mass balance (Dowdeswell *et al.* 2008). Calving constitutes about 40 per cent of mass loss at both Devon Ice Cap and Prince of Wales Ice Fields in the Canadian Arctic (Burgess and Sharp 2008, Mair *et al.* 2009). Calving and melt from glaciers and ice caps can also result in more rapid basin-wide thinning than on ice sheets because of glaciers' and small ice caps' smaller reservoir size relative to the size of the marine outlet. Researchers are still trying to understand if these data indicate a trend.

For example, the mass loss from a 39,000 square kilometre region in Alaska's St. Elias mountains during 2003-2007 was about 21 km^3 per year, making the basin-averaged thinning rate 0.5 metres per year (Arendt *et al.* 2009). In comparison, Greenland's mass loss for approximately the same period was 180 km^3 per year, taken from a total of 1,7 million square kilometres; the basin-averaged thinning rate is 0.01 metres per year, smaller than the St. Elias thinning rate by a factor of 50. Similarly, the calving flux from Alaska's Columbia Glacier in 2001-2005 was 7 km^3 per year from a basin 750 square kilometres in area, with a resulting basin-averaged thinning of 9.3 metres per year. Jakobshavn Isbrae in Greenland presently discharges about 24 km^3 per year from a basin of 92,000 square kilometres, with a resulting basin-averaged thinning rate of 0.25 metres per year, 37 times less than Columbia's thinning rate (Meier *et al.* 2007). Again, while Greenland has a much larger reservoir of ice and consequently potential contribution to sea-level rise than do glaciers and ice caps, glaciers and ice caps have the potential to change volume much faster in the coming decades to centuries (Meier *et al.* 2007).

Evidence of glacier loss has been documented on every continent using different methods to measure rates of change. In 1894, the entire area of glaciers in the Pyrenees was mapped and measured for the first time, with the Spanish portion covering 1779 hectares. Measurements were not taken again until 1982, when the area of Spanish Pyrenean glaciers had shrunk to 595 hectares. In 1993, only 468 glacier-covered hectares were measurable and in 2003, only 277 hectares remained (ERHIN 2009). Measurements from 2008 showed glacier extent covering only 260 hectares in the Spanish Pyrenees, with the researchers suggesting that if current trends continue, glaciers will disappear from the Pyrenees by 2050 (González *et al.* 2008).

Most icecaps and glaciers in the mountains of tropical Africa are expected to disappear by 2030 (Eggermont *et al.* 2007, Hastenrath 2009). Loss

Table 2.1: Decline of Pyrenean glaciers 1894-2008

(Figures in hectares)								
Year	1894	1982	1991	1994	1998	1999	2001	2008
Balaitus	55	18	15	13	5	2	0	0.5
Infierno	88	62?	66	55	43	41	41	40.7
Viñemal	40	20	18	17	8	6	2	1.2
Taillón	-	10	2	2	1	<1	0	0
M. Perdido	556	107	90	74	52	48	44	36.6
La Munia	40	12	10	8	3	0	0	6.7
Posets	216	55	48	48	35	34	34	28.2
Perdiguero	92	10?	17	9	<1	0	0	-
Aneto-Mal	692	314	302	249	169	163	162	152
Besiberri	-	-	6	6	6	6	6	-
TOTAL	1779	608	574	481	322	300	290	<260

Numbers of glaciers and ice banks						
Year	1980	1991	1994	1999	2000	2008
Glaciers	27	17	13	10	10	10
Ice banks	9	19	19	16	9	9
TOTAL	36	36	32	26	19	19

Source: González et al. 2008, ERHIN 2009

Quelccaya ice cap of Qori Kalis Glacier in 1978 (left) and in 2004 (right). *Source: L.Thompson*

of permanent ice from Africa's mountains will have profound effects on surrounding ecosystems, as well as the hydrology and temperature regime of Africa's unique highland cold-water lakes. Efforts have begun to document the baseline climatic, environmental, and biological conditions in Africa's mountains to evaluate future changes. Sediments accumulating on the bottom of highland glacial lakes have chronicled the history of central African climate and environmental dynamics, producing the historical perspective needed for resource conservation and responsible adaptation. Surveys of lake sediments in the Rwenzori Mountains show that recent glacier recession started around 1880, broadly coinciding in timing with declining East African rainfall. The data do not show glacial expansion coinciding with the initiation of this wet phase in the early 19th century, highlighting the complexity of the relationship between tropical glaciers and climate (Eggermont *et al.* 2007).

Repeat photography of some of the earliest glacier images from southern South America reveals drastic, widespread glacier recession in northwestern Patagonia between 38° and 45°S. Linear trends in regionally-averaged annual and seasonal temperature and precipitation records indicate substantial warming and decreasing precipitation over the 1912–2002 interval. Regionally-averaged mean annual stream flow records east of the Andes mountains show a highly significant negative correlation with the regional temperature series. Given the major socio-economic importance of rivers and glaciers in this area, potential impacts of the future warmer and drier climates projected for this region will be considerable (Masiokas *et al.* 2008).

Naimona'nyi's frozen ice. *Source: T. Nash* ©

For the most part, land-terminating glaciers of western Canada and the northwestern United States have retreated since the 19th century, although average rates of retreat varied in the first half of the 20th century, with glaciers stabilizing or even advancing until 1980 and then resuming consistent recession. This most recent retreat has been accompanied by statistically detectable declines in late-summer streamflow from glacier-fed catchments over much of the area, although there is some geographical variation. In many valleys, glacier retreat has produced geomorphic hazards, including outburst floods from moraine-dammed lakes, mass failures from over-steepened valley walls, and debris flows generated on moraines. With the climate projected to continue warming over the 21st century, current trends in hydrology, geomorphology, and water quality should continue, with a range of implications for water resource availability and management, and for river ecosystems (Moore *et al.* 2009).

Ice cores collected in 2006 from Naimona'nyi Glacier in the Himalaya of the Tibetan Plateau lack distinctive marker horizons, suggesting no net accumulation of ice mass since at least 1950. Naimona'nyi is the highest glacier documented to be losing mass annually, suggesting the possibility of similar mass loss on other high-elevation glaciers in low and mid-latitudes under a warmer Earth scenario. If climatic conditions dominating the mass balance of Naimona'nyi extend to other glaciers in the region, the implications for water resources could be serious as these glaciers feed the headwaters of the Indus, Ganges, and Brahmaputra Rivers that sustain one of the world's most populous regions (Kehrwald *et al.* 2008).

In the Himalaya particularly, glacier loss increases the threat of glacier lake outburst floods. Often, mountain glaciers leave a front moraine at their former terminus that can contain the glacier's melting run-off in a pro-glacial lake. Reservoirs for hydroelectric facilities may have a similar configuration. When a moraine or other type of barrier is breached, the full contents of the lake may descend through the downstream valley as a torrent. The breach can occur because the lake has filled too much, high winds have forced water over the barrier, or a large wave results from sudden collapse of ice at the glacier front or sidewall debris. The result can tear out bottomland, forests, settlements, and hydroelectric power installations very quickly (Chaudhary and Aryal 2009).

Himalayan glaciers are retreating at rates between 10 and 60 metres per year. The terminus of most high valley glaciers in Bhutan, Nepal, and neighbouring parts of China are retreating very fast. Vertical shifts over the last fifty years of 100 metres have been recorded and retreat rates of 30 metres per year have become common. Particular situations with glacier lake outburst flood potential are under observation: These include Nepal's Lake Imja Tsho in the Khumbu-Everest region—where the Imja glacier is retreating at 74 metres per year, and Bhutan's Pho Chu Basin where

Figure 2.2: Arctic sea-ice extent October 16, 2009

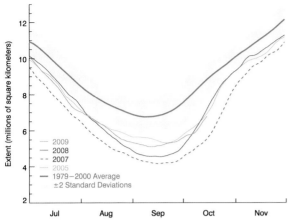

2009 Arctic sea-ice extent (area of ocean with at least 15 per cent sea-ice) compared to recent years. *Source: NSIDC 2009a*

some pro-glacial lakes have increased in size by 800 per cent. In the Pho Chu Basin several lakes are interconnected and a significant event at the top could cascade throughout the system (ICIMOD 2007, ICIMOD 2009).

ARCTIC ICE

Polar scientists use satellite imagery and other observations that show the Arctic ice cover is declining more rapidly than estimated by any of the computer models used by the IPCC in preparing its 2007 assessments (Stroeve *et al.* 2007, Overland 2009, Wang and Overland 2009, Johannessen 2008). While natural variability plays a significant role in Arctic sea-ice extent, radiative forcing from anthropogenic sources is growing in influence (Serreze *et al.* 2007, Stroeve *et al.* 2007). In 2008 and 2009 the extent of Arctic sea-ice was well below the 1979-2000 average. This might be associated with higher air and ocean temperatures and changes in particular ocean circulation patterns (Stroeve *et al.* 2008, Giles *et al.* 2008, Wang and Overland 2009, Kwok *et al.* 2009).

In 2007, the sea-ice in the Arctic Ocean shrank to its smallest extent on record, 24 per cent less than the previous record set in 2005 and 34 per cent less than the average minimum extent over 1970-2000 (ESA 2007, Comiso *et al.* 2008, Stroeve *et al.* 2008). The minimum sea-ice cover of 2007 extended over 4,52 million square kilometres of the Arctic Ocean (NSIDC 2009a). This is clear evidence of a phenomenon of importance on a planetary scale forced by global warming and caused mainly by an Earth System energy imbalance due to GHG concentrations increasing in the atmosphere (IPY 2009).

Mooserboden reservoir in Carpathia, Austria, part of the Kaprun hydroelectric plant looking southwards. *Source: P. Himsworth*

Arctic sea-ice coverage in 2008 finished with the second-lowest minimum extent in the satellite record, 9 per cent above the 2007 minimum. However, the Arctic summer of 2008 experienced different wind and ocean circulation patterns compared to 2007, resulting in a more diffuse ice cover and a thinner pack: This suggests a record low volume of Arctic sea-ice at the end of summer 2008 (NSIDC 2009a).

The nature of the Arctic sea-ice cover has changed drastically over the last few decades, with much more extensive proportions of first- and second-year ice. In 1988, 21 per cent of the sea-ice cover was 7+ years old and 31 per cent was 5+ years old. In 2007, only 5 per cent was 7+ years old and 10 per cent was 5+ years old. Within the central Arctic Basin in 1987, 57 per cent of the ice pack was 5+ years old and at least 14 per cent was 9+ years old. The Arctic Basin in 2007 had only 7 per cent of ice coverage 5+ years old and no ice that was 9 years or older (Maslanik *et al.* 2007, Haas *et al.* 2008).

As the melt season of 2009 began, the Arctic Ocean was covered mostly by first-year ice, which formed since September 2008, and second-year ice, which formed during the winter of 2007 to 2008. First-year ice in particular is thinner and prone to melt more quickly than thicker multi-year ice. In 2009, ice older than two years accounted for less than 10 per cent of the ice cover at the end of February (NSIDC 2009a). This is quite a significant decline considering that only a decade ago, older ice on average accounted for 30 per cent the total sea-ice cover at the same time of the year. Ultimately, thinner and more vulnerable Arctic sea-ice has profound implications for the global climate system, as ice cover serves to naturally cool air and water masses, and plays a key role in ocean circulation and reflecting solar radiation back into space.

Two ocean circulation patterns dominate the Arctic Ocean: The Transpolar Drift moves water and ice from the region of the East Siberian Sea along the north of Eurasia and over the North Pole to drain into the deep Fram Strait between Greenland and Svalbard. The Beaufort Gyre circles between the North Pole and the coast of northwestern Canada and Alaska, rotating in a clockwise direction and fostering the growth of multi-year ice as floes circle for many years.

Box 2.1: International Polar Year

From March 1, 2007 until February 25, 2009 over 10,000 scientists from 60 nations participated in facets of an international multidisciplinary research collaboration known as the International Polar Year (IPY). The IPY's coordination and integration of ongoing research projects, as well as exploiting the opportunity to fill in scientific gaps, is attempting to fill the demand for up-to-date scientific interpretations of how climate in the Arctic and Antarctic is changing. As a group, IPY scientists made a statement about the record low sea-ice extent in the Arctic:

"Our main conclusions so far indicate that there is a very low probability that Arctic sea ice will ever recover. As predicted by all IPCC models, Arctic sea ice is more likely to disappear in summer in the near future. However it seems like this is going to happen much sooner than models predicted, as pointed out by recent observations and data reanalysis undertaken during IPY and the Damocles Integrated Project. The entire Arctic system is evolving to a new super interglacial stage seasonally ice free, and this will have profound consequences for all the elements of the Arctic cryosphere, marine and terrestrial ecosystems and human activities. Both the atmosphere and the ocean circulation and stratification (ventilation) will also be affected. This raises a critical set of issues, with many important implications potentially able to speed up melting of the Greenland ice sheet, accelerating the rise in sea-levels and slowing down the world ocean conveyor belt. That would also have a lot of consequences on the ocean carbon sink and ocean acidification."

Source: IPY 2009

Figure 2.3: Beaufort Gyre and Transpolar Drift currents

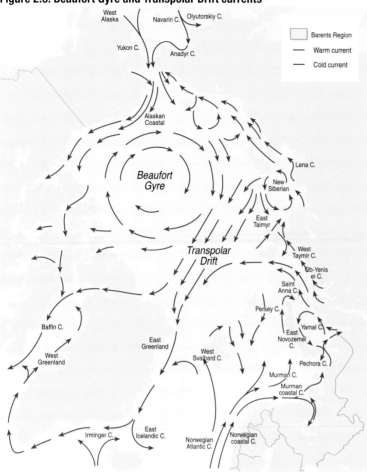

The wind-driven Arctic ice circulation pattern has two primary components. First, the Beaufort Gyre is a clockwise circulation in the Beaufort Sea, north of Alaska. This circulation results from an average high-pressure system that spawns winds over the region. A second component is the Transpolar Drift Stream, where ice moves from the Siberian coast of Russia, across the Arctic basin, exiting into the North Atlantic off the east coast of Greenland.
Source: UNEP/GRID-Arendal 1998

During the last few decades of the 20th century, the positive phase of the Northern Annular Mode (NAM)—an encompassing category that includes Arctic Oscillation and North Atlantic Oscillation states—produced conditions that strengthened Arctic Ocean winds transporting ice away from the Alaskan and Siberian coasts via the Transpolar Drift and flushing large amounts out of the Arctic Basin through the Fram Strait and into the North Atlantic (Serreze et al. 2007). The Transpolar Drift seemed to veer powerfully over the Pole and pick up more ice off the northern edge of the Beaufort Gyre for years, exporting multi-year ice before it could return to the Canada Basin and Beaufort Sea for another annual accumulation of additional ice. By the beginning of the 21st century, the NAM had returned to a more neutral state and multi-year ice accumulated again in the Arctic Basin.

However in 2007, positive NAM conditions prevailed over the summer and once again multi-year ice continued to drain from the Arctic Basin (Maslanik et al. 2007, Serreze et al. 2007, Kwok et al. 2009, NSIDC 2009a). Based on sea-ice age data from researchers at the University of Colorado, during the winter of 2008/2009, 390,000 square kilometres of second-year ice and 190,000 square kilometres of older (more than two years old) ice moved out of the Arctic (NSIDC 2009a).

Researchers recognize the gradual long-term warming over the last 30 years, mostly characterized by milder winter freezing seasons and longer summer melting seasons,

evidencing strong reflectivity or positive albedo feedback effects. Less ice means more open water exposed to shortwave solar radiation that would be absorbed and transformed into heat. Strong positive feedback accelerates the melting of Arctic sea-ice, largely due to the sharp contrast of the high albedo for sea-ice areas covered with snow that reflects 80 per cent of the incoming solar radiation back into space, in contrast with the very low albedo of the ocean that reflects only 20 per cent of the solar radiation, absorbing the other 80 per cent (Graversen et al. 2008, Dmitrenko et al. 2008).

Natural variability in atmospheric and ocean circulation patterns combined with radiative forcing to shrink the 2007 ice extent so much. Over the western Arctic Ocean in 2007, observations estimate total summertime cloud cover decreased by 16 per cent from 2006 to 2007. Over three months of 24 hour sunlight under clear skies, the total radiative forcing warmed the surface ocean by 2.4 degrees Celsius, enhancing basal ice melt. Both an increase of air temperatures and a decrease in relative humidity, associated with the persistent clockwise atmospheric circulation pattern, explain the reduced cloudiness (Kay et al. 2008).

Major efforts since 2002 to document the nature of the Beaufort Gyre have reported significant differences between the climatology of the 1990s and the observed phenomenon characterizing post-2003 conditions. The Beaufort Gyre contains significant amounts of fresh water within its ice floes, but also within its circulating water column. Since the 1990s the Gyre has reduced in surface area but gained up to 1,000 square kilometres of additional fresh water since the 2000s began by tightening and accelerating its circulation pattern (Proshutinsky et al. 2009). Freshwater sources in the Arctic include flow from the Pacific Ocean, precipitation, ice melt, and discharge from major river systems including the Ob, Yenisey, and Lena of Russia and the Mackenzie of Canada. Scientists assumed that Arctic fresh water flowed from the basin in balance with the input from the various sources until observations showed large discrepancies between the two estimates. More recently, researchers suggest that fresh water is stored within Arctic circulation systems under certain conditions and is then released when those conditions dissipate (Proshutinsky et al.

Figure 2.4: Trend in winter multi-year and first-year sea-ice fractions

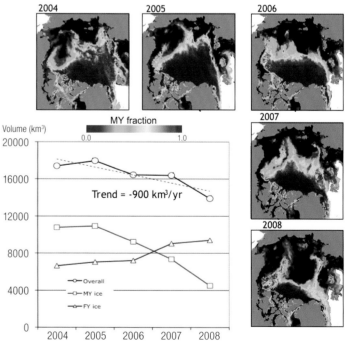

Satellite measurements of winter multi-year ice cover in the Arctic Ocean between 2004 and 2008, along with the corresponding downward trend in overall winter sea-ice volume, and switch in dominant ice type from multi-year ice to first-year ice.
Source: Kwok et al. 2009

2008, McPhee *et al.* 2009, Proshutinsky *et al.* 2009). Scientists from the Norwegian Polar Institute warn that fresh water is piling up in the Arctic Ocean and that a change in the dominant wind direction could release the largest amount of fresh water through Fram Strait ever recorded (NPI 2009, Holfort *et al.* 2009).

Before the 2007 summer, most models for seasonal ice loss envisioned an ice-free September for the Arctic Ocean in the waning years of the 21st century (Serreze *et al.* 2006, Boé *et al.* 2009). The plummeting sea-ice extent of 2007 demanded new analyses and suggested new trends. Researchers who track the growth and melt of polar ice found the longterm outlook 'disturbing', particularly because all the models used for the IPCC AR4 underestimated the timing of Arctic ice loss (Stroeve *et al.* 2007, Stroeve *et al.* 2008). They suggest this may be due to an assumption of sea-ice thickness in the models greater than existed in reality (Stroeve *et al.* 2008). A reconsideration of the trends led to speculation that the Arctic Ocean may be ice-free in September by 2030.

The continuing sparse ice extent recorded in September 2008 spurred further analysis: At current rates of coverage, more than 60 per cent of the Arctic Ocean area is open to increased solar irradiation at the end of summer and temperatures in the Arctic autumn now reach 5-6 degrees Celsius above the climatological norm (Wang and Overland 2009, Overland 2009). From examination of models that most closely match the observation of summer Arctic sea-ice loss including 2007 and 2008, these researchers suggest that the Arctic could be virtually ice-free in September of 2037 (Wang and Overland 2009). Furthermore, they posit that with summers like 2007, a nearly ice-free September by 2028 is well within the realm of possibility.

The confidence behind these projections of rapidly decreasing Arctic summer sea-ice is based in those same models: Some indicate rapid ice cover decrease once the areal extent of the ice cover shrinks to vulnerable dimensions (Serreze and Francis 2006, Stroeve *et al.* 2008, Wang and Overland 2009).

Some Arctic sea-ice loss simulations suggest a different sequence of possible future events: A gradual transition to a seasonally ice-free Arctic Ocean and then a shift to a year-round ice-free state (Delworth *et al.* 2008, Delworth *et al.* 2006). Earlier models showed this possible shift to year-round ice-free conditions could happen either gradually or abruptly (Winton 2006). New research supports a seasonally ice-free Arctic with some stability: The thermodynamic effects of sea-ice mitigate the possibility of sudden ice loss when the Arctic Ocean is ice covered during a sufficiently large fraction of the year. These results suggest that critical threshold behaviour is unlikely as perennial sea-ice conditions develop to seasonally ice-free conditions. However, these models still allow that a critical threshold associated with the sudden loss of the remaining wintertime-only sea-ice cover may exist (Eisenman and Wettlaufer 2009).

From September of 2006 until January of 2008, the research schooner Tara—sponsored by the European Union Programme: Developing Arctic Modeling and Observing Capabilities for Long-term Environmental Studies (DAMOCLES)—travelled on the Transpolar Drift to reproduce the 1894-1896 Fram expedition led by Fritdjof Nansen. Tara drifted closer to the North Pole than Fram had, and surprisingly Tara completed the transect from the Laptev Sea to the Fram Strait in 15 months while the drift carried the Fram that distance in 3 years. In September of 2007, the Russian vessel Akademik Fedorov deployed a drifting station near the Severnaya Zemlya Russian islands. That drifting station was recovered near Svalbard ten months later, confirming the acceleration of the transpolar drift as also observed by Tara (IPY 2009). A series of buoys dropped on Transpolar Drift ice in 2001, 2004, and 2007 followed through on research begun in 1991 that verified the ice travelling through

Figure 2.5: Arctic rivers and their discharge (km³/year)

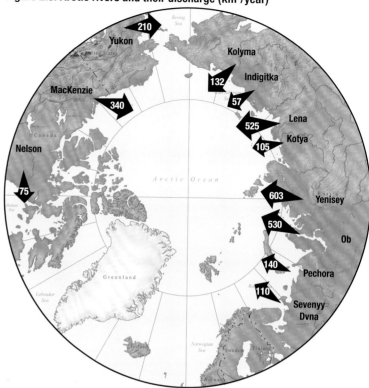

Source: CAFF 2001

the drift has become first- and second-year ice in recent years while the earlier observations showed older ice was previously common in the system (Haas *et al.* 2008).

The Canadian Arctic Archipelago (CAA) is also changing rapidly. In a study following data from 1979-2008, the average September total sea-ice

Box 2.2: Implications of sea-ice loss

The implications of so little multi-year ice in the Arctic are now being investigated. First-year ice melts more quickly, so larger areas of open water will be exposed to solar radiation earlier in the year, which will increase both sea and atmospheric temperatures. The larger heat transfer from the ocean to the atmosphere—the maritime effect—will help moderate autumn and winter cold temperatures. As ice retreats from shorelines, winds gain a longer fetch over open water, resulting in stronger waves and increased shore erosion.

Accelerated sea-ice loss will not only affect the Arctic Ocean coast. The rapid retreat of Arctic sea-ice could accelerate rapid warming 1,500 kilometres inland throughout Alaska, Canada, and Russia. During rapid ice retreat, the rate of inland warming could be more than three times that previously suggested by global climate models.

Such drastic changes in climate will affect ecosystems and the human populations that depend on them. While higher temperatures are radically changing the environment in the North, they also will thaw out extensive expanses of permafrost, defined as earth that remains frozen for two or more consecutive years. The more apparent effects will include damaged infrastructure as roads, pipelines, and foundations collapse, as well as 'drunken forests' that result from altered rooting conditions. More serious complications result from the potential release of methane and carbon dioxide that are currently frozen in Arctic soils. The expected rapid soil thaw could also produce a talik—a layer of permanently unfrozen soil sandwiched between the seasonally frozen layer above and the perennially frozen layer below—which in turn creates a more rapid heat build-up in the soil, further accelerating the longterm thaw and release of carbon dioxide (Lawrence *et al.* 2009, UNEP 2008c, Serreze *et al.* 2007, Jones *et al.* 2009, Jones *et al.* 2008, Mars and Houseknecht 2007).

area within the CAA has decreased by 8.7 per cent each decade, while the melt season duration is increasing significantly at 7 days per decade. The longest melt season of the full thirty years lasted 129 days in 2008. The CAA is on the receiving end of the multi-year ice delivery from the interactions of the Transpolar Drift and the Beaufort Gyre, but even there the average September multi-year ice area is decreasing by 6.4 per cent per decade. The Northwest Passage, touted as a future shortcut between the North Atlantic and the Pacific, will continue to be susceptible to multi-year ice blocking the Western Parry Channel region as the transition to a sea-ice free Arctic summer continues, limiting the dependability of transiting through the CAA (Howell *et al.* 2009).

In the early 20th century, explorers of Canada's Ellesmere Island described a glacial front skirting the island's northern coast. Modern glaciologists have deduced that this ice front was likely a continuous ice shelf covering some 89,000 square kilometres. By the 1950s, much of that ice had disintegrated. Retreating glaciers which formerly fed the vast amalgamated shelf differentiated and lost contact with each other. That retreat and differentiation, together with the reduced protection once sea-ice loss took effect, contributed to the now almost complete disintegration of Ellesmere island ice shelves (England *et al.* 2008, Mueller *et al.* 2008, Scott 2008).

The loss of sea-ice in the Arctic Ocean will have serious repercussions as feedbacks from temperature increases, altered seasons, and shifting circulation patterns cascade through Arctic biophysical systems. But the loss of Arctic Ocean sea-ice will not directly lead to any significant sea-level rise because all the ice is already floating. Ice shelves on surrounding coastlines and glaciers that reach inland and deliver ice to the oceans will experience additional melt from the warmer temperatures (England *et al.* 2008). Inland and outlet glaciers will continue to contribute to sea-level rise. Observations over the past decades show a rapid acceleration of several outlet glaciers in Greenland and Antarctica.

OUTLET GLACIERS IN TRANSITION

Among the various oceanographic, hydrological, atmospheric, and ecological consequences of changes in the volume of the Earth's land ice, the forecasting of future sea level stands as arguably the most globally significant. One process by which sea level is increased is by the addition

Russian vessel Akademik Fedorov. *Source: N. Harrison*

of new water mass from land ice. This transfer can occur by melting of ice from direct climatological forcing, but also by the flow of glacier ice mass into oceans and calving of icebergs into the ocean—aspects of glacier dynamics. Glacier dynamics can produce extremely rapid increases in sea level because increasing glacier flow and iceberg calving do not track increasing temperature in a simple way, but sometimes respond non-linearly and irreversibly to climate inputs. Past dynamic contributions to sea level have long been hypothesized from geologic evidence, while the possibility of rapid dynamic response of ice sheets to climate change has been under consideration since the 1970s. Most research on rapid dynamic changes since that time, including rapid iceberg discharge, has been conducted on glaciers and ice caps; however, somewhat in the past decade but especially since the IPCC AR4, research on dynamics of ice sheets, as well as glacier and ice cap dynamics, has increased sharply (Zwally *et al.* 2002, Pfeffer 2007, Benn *et al.* 2007, Howat *et al.* 2008, Briner *et al.* 2009). Understanding of the mechanisms and controls on rapid dynamic-forced changes in glacier and ice sheet contributions to sea level is now among the most urgently pursued goals in glaciology and sea-level investigations. The notable absence of predictions of a dynamic-forced component of sea-level rise from the IPCC AR4 made their sea-level predictions a very conservative lower-bound estimate (IPCC 2007b).

Two main hypotheses guide current research to explain the acceleration of outlet glaciers in Greenland, Antarctica, and at the marine boundaries of other glaciers and ice caps. The first suggests that dynamic changes result from processes that act to destabilize marine-ending termini and disrupt force balances that persist up the glacier. This destabilization then leads to faster ice flow and thinning that propagates rapidly up-glacier and leads to further retreat (Pfeffer 2007, Sole *et al.* 2008). The second hypothesis is that warmer air temperatures accelerate sliding by increasing the amount of surface melt. Some fraction of surface water may percolate through the ice mass and, once it reaches the glacier bed, increases basal lubrication and the rate at which ice slides over its bed. This leads to glacier acceleration, thinning, and terminus retreat. This mechanism would behave similarly on both land and marine terminating outlet glaciers (Parizek and Alley 2005, Sole *et al.* 2008).

GREENLAND ICE

The recent marked retreat, thinning, and acceleration of most of Greenland's outlet glaciers south of 70° N has increased concerns over contributions from the Greenland Ice Sheet to future sea-level rise (Howat *et al.* 2005). These rapid changes seem to be parallel to the warming trend in Greenland, the mechanisms are poorly understood.

An analysis of a large sample of southern Greenland Ice Sheet marine- and land-terminating outlet glacier thinning rates showed that more than 75 per cent of marine-terminating outlet glaciers are thinning significantly more than their land-terminating counterparts. There was a dramatic

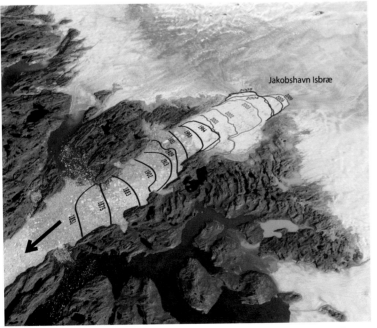

Jakobshavn Glacier in western Greenland has been rapidly losing ice from its terminus for more than a decade due to warm water currents reaching up the fjord. The arrow indicates direction of discharge, while the glacier retreats back towards the Greenland Ice Sheet. *Source: NASA 2009*

increase in almost all marine outlet glacier thinning rates from 1993 to 2006, when the documentation ended, suggesting a widespread forcing mechanism. These findings suggest that a change in a controlling mechanism specific to the thinning rates of marine-terminating outlet glaciers occurred in the late 1990s and that this change did not affect thinning rates of land-terminating outlet glaciers (Sole *et al.* 2008).

A study of Helheim Glacier, a large outlet glacier on Greenland's eastern coast, used an ice flow model to reproduce the changes documented for the glacier's recent dynamics. The researchers found the ice acceleration, thinning, and retreat began at the calving terminus and then propagated upstream along the glacier. They could not detect any relationships between surface ice melt or drainage and any subsequent changes in ice dynamics. They concluded that the changes were unlikely to be caused by basal lubrication through surface melt propagating to the glacier bed. While the researchers confirmed that tidewater outlet glaciers adjust extremely rapidly to changing boundary conditions at the terminus, they could not determine any boundary condition change that initiated the terminus' instability and concluded that recent rates of mass loss in Greenland's outlet glaciers are transient and should not be extrapolated into the future (Nick *et al.* 2009).

Another study focused on western Greenland's Jakobshavn Isbrae responsible for draining 7 per cent of the ice sheet's area, which switched from slow thickening to rapid thinning in 1997 and suddenly doubled its velocity. Here, the change in glacier dynamics is also attributed to destabilization of the glacier terminus, but the researchers are able to attribute that to warmer ocean water delivered to the fjord. However, these researchers were also able to detect short-term and less significant fluctuations in Jakobshavn Isbrae's behaviour that could be attributed to meltwater drainage events (Holland *et al.* 2008).

They present hydrographic data documenting a sudden increase in subsurface ocean temperature along the entire west coast of Greenland in the 1990s that reached Jakobshavn Isbrae's fjord in 1997. The researchers trace the warm flow back to the east of Greenland where the subpolar gyre that rotates counter clockwise south of Iceland scoops warmer water from an extension of the Gulf Stream and directs it back west and south around the tip of southern Greenland. In the early 1990s the North Atlantic Oscillation atmospheric pattern switched phase and drove the subpolar gyre closer to the Greenland shore, accelerating the flow of the warm water around the tip and up the western shore, where it eventually reached the Jakobshavn Isbrae fjord (Holland *et al.* 2008). The delivery of warm water to the base of Jakobshavn Isbrae's fjord persisted through 2007 and the retreat continued at least through 2008, with shorter term fluctuations affected by surface melt permeating through the ice mass (Holland *et al.* 2008, Box *et al.* 2009). Whether this pulse of warm water from the subpolar gyre also affected Helheim and other marine outlet glaciers in Greenland will have to be investigated.

Such studies not only illuminate the dynamics of outlet glaciers in a changing environment and subject to a variety of forcings, they also help us understand the significance of particular topographical configurations beneath ice that certainly affect current phenomena and could play a strong role in future events. Both Helheim and Jakobshavn occupy deep valleys that extend far into Greenland's inland territory. The possibility remains, for these and similarly configured outlet glaciers, that should they lose their ice plugs they would act as drainage outlets for Greenland's interior meltwater. Given the many interacting variables affecting the Earth's ice in a changing climate, the future behaviour of these large outlet glaciers remains unpredictable (Holland *et al.* 2008, Nick *et al.* 2009).

Figure 2.6: Seasonal melt departure and maximum temperature anomaly in Greenland

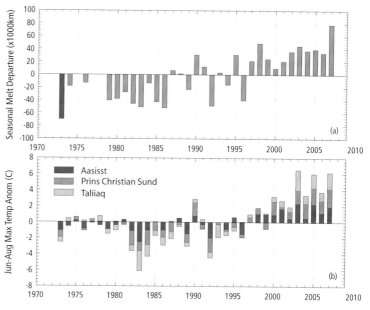

(a) Seasonal Melt Departure (SMD) for June-August and (b) seasonal maximum daily temperature anomalies at three coastal meteorological stations in Greenland for June-August from 1973 to 2007. *Source: Mote 2007*

Many other outlet glaciers in Greenland are in retreat from disturbance at terminus and because of meltwater permeating their mass. In 2008, researchers reported on one of the thousands of melt-water lakes that now form on Greenland each summer. The four-kilometre-wide expanse of water that formed in 2006 completely drained into the icy depths in 90 minutes, at a flow rate greater than Niagara Falls (Joughin *et al.* 2008, Das *et al.* 2008). The latest documentation has shown that this particular surface melt drainage event fed into the Jakobshavn Basin behind the glacier terminus (Mottram *et al.* 2009).

The Greenland Ice Sheet

The nature of Greenland Ice Sheet surface melt is also under examination and it seems to be accelerating: A time series of Greenland surface melt extent, frequency, and onset has been updated to include data from 1973 to 2007, when the documentation ended. The seasonal melt departure, the sum from 1 June to 31 August of the departure from average of each day's melt extent, is a new metric used to describe the amount of melt. Results show a large increase in melt in summer 2007, 60 per cent more than the previous high in 1998. During summer 2007, some locations south of 70°N had as many as 50 more days of melt than average. Melt occurred as much as 30 days earlier than average. The seasonal melt departure is shown to be significantly related to coastal temperatures as monitored by meteorological stations, although 2007 had more melt than might be expected, based on the summer temperature record (Mote 2007).

ANTARCTIC ICE

The very high average elevation, about 2,300 metres above sea level, of the Antarctic Ice Sheet and continuous latitudinal ring of open ocean separating Antarctica from other landmasses isolates the ice sheet from warmer latitudes to the north. Prevailing westerly winds encircling Antarctica match a circulation pattern in the Southern Ocean, the Antarctic Circumpolar Current (ACC), which is the Earth's fastest moving current and is only constrained as it passes from the Pacific to the Atlantic through the Drake Passage. Non-synchronous and multidecadal influences—from the westerlies, the ACC, pressure systems that build over the Southern Ocean, and the amount of fresh water draining from the continent—all affect fluctuations of Antarctica's ice (Mayewski *et al.* 2009).

Lake Fryxell in the Transatlantic Mountains. *Source: Joe Mastroanni/ National Science Foundation (NSF)*

Parts of Antarctica are also losing ice, particularly from the West Antarctic Ice Sheet. Researchers estimate that loss of ice from West Antarctica increased by 60 per cent in the decade to 2006. Ice loss from the Antarctic Peninsula, which extends from West Antarctica towards South America, increased by 140 per cent. The processes affecting the peninsula involve accelerating glacier flows caused by both warmer air and higher ocean temperatures (Rignot *et al.* 2008). An additional factor in West Antarctica and the Antarctic Peninsula that could undermine the integrity of the great ice sheets is the recent disappearance of a number of ice shelves that build along those shores.

Box 2.3: Relationships between stratospheric ozone and climate change

Integrating the effects of changing stratospheric ozone concentrations with climate models remains a challenge for Earth System scientists. However, new research and experimentation are revealing the wide range of influence that stratospheric ozone depletion has on temperatures in the upper troposphere that can propagate downward. In the troposphere, and reaching to the Earth's surface, this influence may reach to affecting the speed of the Southern Westerlies, the strength of cyclonic circulation in the Southern Ocean, the extent of Antarctic sea-ice, and the possibility of upwelling that releases carbon dioxide from deep ocean reservoirs. Stratospheric ozone depletion is partly responsible for masking expected warmth in Antarctica, and successful ozone recovery will lead to the projected increase in Antarctic temperatures.

Total ozone measured in Dobson units: September 4, 2009

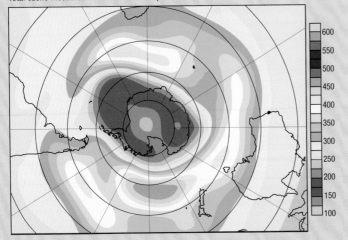

Source: Shindell and Schmidt 2004, Forster et al. 2007, Son et al. 2008, Shindell 2008, Turner et al. 2009, Toggweiler 2009, Anderson et al. 2009, Toggweiler and Russell 2008.

These shelves are immense—the Ross ice shelf is the largest and is slightly smaller than Spain. The shelves are already floating on the ocean so their loss does not add to sea-level rise. But they are attached to the ice sheets and act as buttresses (BAS 2008). When they go, the ice sheets may accelerate out into the ocean and that does displace the water. Ice shelves also act as buffer areas between the changes in temperature and winds over open waters of the Southern Ocean and the more subdued weather systems of Antarctica's interior.

A large part of the 13,000 square kilometre Wilkins Ice Shelf, between 70° and 74°W along the Antarctic Peninsula, collapsed in February 2008 (Braun *et al.* 2008). At that time the British Antarctic Survey said the shelf was in imminent danger of disintegration because it seemed to be stabilized only by a slim ice bridge that extended between two islands (BAS 2008). Finally, in early April 2009, that ice bridge broke and throughout the Antarctic winter the shelf has been sheering into huge slivered bergs that are slowly moving away from the mainland (ESA 2009). The collapse of the Wilkins Ice Shelf will not directly lead to sea-level rise but the event serves as a dire warning: Ice shelves have the potential to become unstable on very short timescales. The collapse of the Wilkins Ice Shelf and its predecessor, the Larsen Ice Shelf which collapsed in 2002, show that, like rapid dynamic response of outlet glaciers, ice shelves can undergo rapid change (Turner *et al.* 2009).

Weather and climate data from Antarctica are difficult to gather because of the size of the region, the logistical difficulties in getting to many areas, and the physical difficulties of working on a continent of ice that is dark and isolated for at least six months every year. As a result, lack of data still remains a significant problem for researchers of Antarctic science. Starting in 1957's International Geophysical Year, data of differing qualities and coverage have been gathered by manned stations, automated weather stations, and satellites. Even today with 42 ground stations in Antarctica, the distribution concentrates along the coasts and paralleling the Transantarctic Mountains to the south of the Ross Ice Shelf. Ground data from the vast interior of the East Antarctic Ice Sheet are still sparse (Steig *et al.* 2009).

In recent decades, traditional assessments of Antarctic temperature change noted the contrast between strong warming around the Antarctic Peninsula and slight cooling of Antarctica's interior (Monaghan *et al.* 2008). This cooling pattern of the interior has been attributed to an increased strength of the circumpolar westerlies reacting to the expansion of the southern subtropical zone moving out from lower latitudes and associated with the depletion of ozone in the stratosphere at those polar latitudes. Without a strong ozone layer at the lower boundary of the stratosphere, the colder stratospheric circulation can propagate downwards to the troposphere and affect surface temperatures over Antarctica and as far north as Patagonia (Thompson and Solomon 2002).

Recent findings show that significant warming extends well to the south of the Antarctic Peninsula to cover most of West Antarctica, an area of warming much larger than previously reported. West Antarctic warming exceeded 0.1°C per decade over the past 50 years, and has been most marked during winter and spring. The whole continent's average near-surface temperature trend is warming, although this is offset somewhat by East Antarctic cooling in autumn (Monaghan *et al.* 2008, Steig *et al.* 2009). These trends appear unrelated to changes in the westerlies; instead, analysis attributes the warming to regional changes in atmospheric circulation and associated changes in sea surface temperature and sea-ice (Steig *et al.* 2009).

Studies of satellite data covering 1987-2006 track how melt is advancing farther inland from the Antarctic coast over this period. Evidence suggests that melt is reaching to higher altitudes and is accelerating on the continent's largest ice shelf (Tedesco *et al.* 2007). This analysis shows when melting began in the different regions with the first evidence along the Peninsula, east from the Peninsula to about 30°E, and then west to the Ross Ice Shelf with detectable melt by 1990.

In contrast to the dramatic decrease in Arctic sea-ice cover, the total area of Antarctic sea-ice has been increasing since the 1970s. At its maximum near the end of the Southern Hemisphere's winter in September, Antarctic sea-ice covers an area of 150,000 square kilometres or more. At maximum extent, southern sea-ice accumulates off the Ross Ice Shelf in the Ross Sea and clots into a rotating mass in the Ross Gyre. Another expansive accumulation grows to the east of the Antarctic Peninsula, in the Weddell Sea.

The Southern Ocean and associated air masses and cryosphere have undergone increased perturbation during recent decades. Ocean station and drifting float observations have revealed rising temperatures in the upper 3,000 metres. Salinity has declined in waters at intermediate depth and the decline may be speeding up in the sparsely sampled latitudes nearest the pole. Sea-ice area increased from 1979 to 1998, particularly in the Ross Sea, while a decline in ice extent since the early 1970s has been led by the Amundsen–Bellingshausen sector. Fresher waters with lower oxygen isotope content on the Pacific–Antarctic continental shelf are consistent with increased melting of continental ice. New bottom water has become colder and less salty downcurrent from that region, but generally warmer in the Weddell Sea. Many ice shelves have retreated or thinned, but others have grown and no trend is apparent in the large iceberg calving rate. Research suggests that ice dynamics in Antarctica are in a state of flux—learning how they are responding to environmental change offers one of the most exciting challenges facing Earth System scientists over the next decade and more (Mayewski et al. 2009).

Many observed Antarctic ice dynamics, especially the increase in sea-ice, have also been linked to the effects of the stratospheric ozone loss (Thompson and Solomon 2002). The effects of the ozone hole extend down through the atmosphere during the summer and autumn so that the greatest increase in surface winds over the Southern Ocean has been during the autumn. However, over approximately the next half century there is expected to be a return to the pre-ozone hole concentrations of ozone, which is expected to bring even warmer temperatures and more dynamic ice conditions (Turner et al. 2009).

Influences on Antarctic climate are becoming more clearly understood, as are the influences that climate has on the whole region. The Earth's ice is responding to warmer temperatures and to a number of complex related processes. Melt from mountain glaciers and ice caps and the Antarctic and Greenland Ice Sheets will continue to contribute to sea-level rise. The question is how much melt will the different sources contribute—and over how long a period?

Figure 2.7: Antarctic temperature trends and sea-ice cover

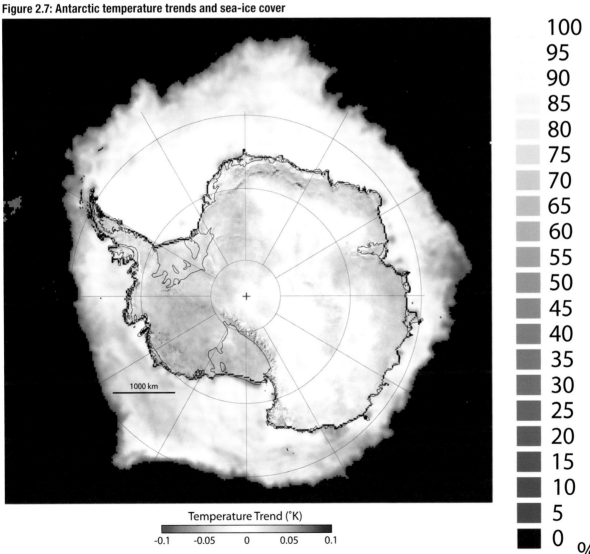

Image shows an overlay of Antarctica's ongoing warming temperature trends (between 1981-2007) and 4 September 2009 sea-ice cover (per cent of total area). *Source: NASA 2007, NSIDC 2009b*

EARTH'S OCEANS

Earth's Oceans

Over the last five decades, the world's oceans have been subjected to fishery overharvesting, seafloor damage from bottom trawling, and habitat loss around margins from coastal development schemes. Climate change further threatens oceans with higher temperatures, increased acidification, and altered circulation and nutrient supplies.

Figure 3.1: Global sea surface temperature anomaly on 10 September, 2009

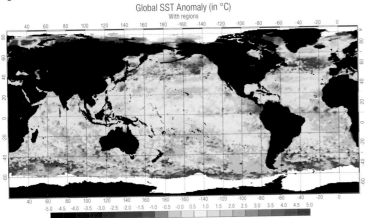

This sea surface temperature (SST) map is generated by subtracting the long-term mean SST, for that location and in that time of year, from the current value. A positive anomaly means that the current sea surface temperature is warmer than average and a negative anomaly means it is cooler than average. *Source: NOAA 2009b*

After 20 years of targeted research into how climate change is affecting Earth Systems, enormous challenges remain in understanding balances, feedbacks, and relations among sub-systems in the world's oceans. Research about sea-level rise, circulation shifts, and chemical responses to anthropogenic inputs often seems to raise more questions than answers.

INCREASED TEMPERATURES

The seasonal variations in heating penetrate into the ocean through a combination of radiation, convective overturning, and mechanical stirring by winds. These processes move heat through the mixed layer, which, on average, involves about 90 metres of the ocean's upper layer. The thermal inertia of a 90 metre layer can add a delay of about six years to the temperature response to an immediate change. With its huge volume and mean depth of about 3,800 metres, the total ocean would take 230 years to fully respond to a temperature change if it were rapidly mixed. However, mixing is not a rapid process for most of the ocean so in reality the response depends on the rate of ventilation of water between the well-mixed upper layers of the ocean and

the deeper, more isolated layers that are separated by the thermocline—the ocean layer exhibiting a strong vertical temperature gradient. The rate of such mixing is not well established and varies greatly geographically. An overall estimate of the delay in surface temperature response caused by the oceans is from 10 to 100 years. The slowest response should be in high latitudes where deep mixing and convection occur, and the fastest response is expected in the tropics. Consequently, the oceans are a great moderating effect on climate changes (Trenberth 2001).

Changes in the climate system's energy budget are predominantly revealed in ocean temperatures and the associated thermal expansion contribution to sea-level rise. Climate models, however, do not reproduce the large decadal variability in globally averaged ocean heat content inferred from the sparse observational database, even when volcanic and other variable climate forcings are included. The sum of the observed contributions has also not adequately explained the overall multi-decadal rise. But now improved estimates of near-global ocean heat content and thermal expansion for the upper 300 metres and 700 metres of the ocean for 1950–2003 have been reported, using statistical techniques that allow for sparse data coverage and that apply corrections to reduce systematic biases in the most common ocean temperature observations. These adjusted ocean warming and thermal expansion trends for 1961–2003 are about 50 per cent larger than earlier estimates but about 40 per cent smaller for 1993–2003, which is consistent with the recognition that previously estimated rates for the 1990s had a positive bias as a result of instrumental errors. On average, the decadal variability of the climate models with volcanic forcing now agrees approximately with the observations, but the modelled multi-decadal trends are smaller than observed (Domingues *et al.* 2008).

SEA-LEVEL RISE

Global average sea level is rising predominantly as a consequence of three factors—thermal expansion of warming ocean water, addition of new water from the ice sheets of Greenland and Antarctica and from glaciers and ice caps, and the addition of water from land surface runoff. All three potential sources are undergoing changes of anthropogenic origin. Regionally, sea level is affected by isostatic responses to the unloading of burden from bedrock, by coastal subsidence in response to removal of materials or to new loads, and by gravitational and ocean current effects causing the ocean surface to deviate from a consistent elevation (Pfeffer *et al.* 2008, Milne *et al.* 2009, Lettenmaier and Milly 2009, Bamber *et al.* 2009).

Since at least the 19th century, sea-level changes have been measured directly by tide gauge records and, since the 1990s, by satellite altimetry. Sea-level changes over longer periods of time, thousands to millions of years, are inferred from geologic evidence (Rohling *et al.* 2009). The average rate of global mean sea-level rise over the 20th century was about 1.7 millimetres (mm) per year. In the period 1993-2003 global mean sea level rose about 3.1 mm per year, and since 2003 the rate of rise has been about 2.5 mm per year. The relative importance of the three factors contributing to global average sea-level rise has varied during this time (Jevrejeva *et al.* 2008, Church 2008, Lettenmaier and Milly 2009, WCRP 2009).

Contributions to sea-level rise are measured by a variety of methods. Synthesis analyses, referred to as sea-level budgets, are conducted periodically

In Hawaii, as in other islands or low-lying regions, sea-level rise combined with high rainfall events pose a flooding risk due to storm sewers backing up with saltwater. Another associated hazard is accelerated beach erosion. *Source: L. Carey*

to compare direct observations of sea-level rise with models and evaluations of the component contributions. Thermal expansion is determined by ocean temperature measurements from large numbers of automated buoys, while glacier and ice sheet contributions are determined by geodetic measurements of land ice volume change as well as by mass budget fluxes observed in individual ice bodies. Since 2003, changes in land ice and land hydrology (surface and underground water flows) have been detected gravitationally by the Gravity Recovery and Climate Experiment (GRACE) satellite system. GRACE observations are also used in combination with satellite altimetry to measure thermal expansion (NASA JPL 2009). Changes in all three components are also estimated by modelling and limited observational data are upscaled to global values by a variety of statistical methods.

Prior to about 1990, ocean thermal expansion accounted for slightly more than 50 per cent of global sea-level rise. Since then, the contribution from thermal expansion has declined to about 15 per cent but this decrease has been countered by increases in glacier, ice cap, and ice sheet contributions. By 2006, glaciers and ice caps contributed about 32 per cent of the total sea-level rise, while the ice sheets on Greenland and Antarctic together contributed about 20 per cent (Milne *et al.* 2009, Hock *et al.* 2009).

While glaciers and ice caps exclusive of the ice sheets dominate present-day contributions to sea-level rise, they collectively constitute a far smaller total sea-level rise owing to their much smaller global volume. If current trends in ice loss continue, the glacier and ice cap reservoir will be exhausted by 2200. On the time scale of decades to the next century, however, glaciers and ice caps will remain a source of sea-level rise equal to or greater than the ice sheets (Meier *et al.* 2007, Bahr *et al.* 2009).

The impacts of sea-level rise will be felt through both an increase in mean sea level and through an increase in the frequency of extreme sea-level events such as storm surges. These impacts include increased frequency and severity of flooding in low-lying areas, erosion of beaches, and damage to infrastructure and the environment, including wetlands and inter-tidal zones, and mangroves, with significant impacts on biodiversity and ecosystem

Figure 3.2: Equivalent water thickness variations over North America

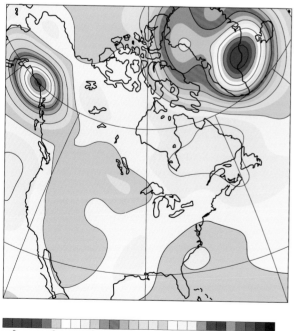

Gravity Recovery and Climate Experiment (GRACE) surface mass-rate field corrected for glacio-isostatic rebound and showing current ice loads of Alaska and Greenland. The twin satellites detect the gravitational fields characterizing different masses on Earth's near surface. *Source: Peltier 2009*

Figure 3.3: What causes sea level to change?

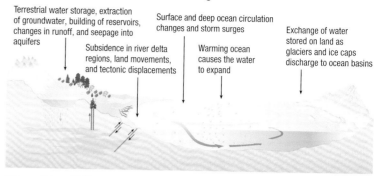

Source: Griggs 2001

Table 3.1: Components of Global Average Sea-Level Rise (millimetres per year)				
Time period	IPCC 2007b 1993-2003	Meier *et al.* 2007, 2006	Cazenave and Nerem 2004, 1993-2003	Cazenave *et al.* 2009, 2003-2008
Thermal expansion	1.6±0.5	—	1.6±0.3	0.34±0.12[3]
Greenland	0.21±0.07	0.50±0.10	0.20±0.04	0.38±0.05
Antarctica	0.21±0.35	0.17±0.11	0.55±0.06	0.56±0.06
Other Glaciers and Ice Caps	0.5±0.18	1.1±0.24	0.8±0.1	1.1±0.25[4]
Land hydrology[5]	—	—	—	0.17±0.1
Sum of components	2.8±0.72[2]	1.8±0.50[1,2]	3.0±0.5[2]	2.2±0.28

Notes:
1: Sum does not include thermal expansion
2: Sum does not include land hydrology
3: Average of two estimates
4: Taken from Meier *et al.* 2007
5: Land hydrology contribution available from GRACE measurements only since 2003

Source: Pfeffer 2009

function. Millions of people in low-lying nations such as Bangladesh, along deltas and river systems like the Mekong, and on islands such as Tuvalu will have to respond to rising sea levels during the 21st century and beyond. Developing and developed countries alike have significant challenges ahead imposed by sea-level rise that will continue for hundreds of years (Church *et al.* 2008, Heberger *et al.* 2009, Karl *et al.* 2009, Solomon *et al.* 2009).

With growing population and infrastructure development human exposure to natural hazards is inevitably increasing. This is particularly true as the strongest population growth is located in coastal areas with greater exposure to floods, cyclones, and high tidal surges. To make matters worse, any land remaining available for urban growth is generally risk-prone, for instance along flood plains or on steep slopes subject to landslides (Nelleman *et al.* 2008). Currently, about 100 million people worldwide live within 1 metre of sea level and that number is growing every day (Anthoff *et al.* 2006).

Infrastructure has been built along many vulnerable coastlines in developing countries, as well as in developed countries, because slopes are gentle enough for buildings, ocean waters are used to cool power plant turbines and industrial processes, and sewage systems discharge to ocean outfalls. Rising sea levels—that will continue to rise for centuries at rates that are not yet well constrained—will be a major determinant in relocating and building new transportation routes, as well as power and waste treatment plants. Relocating business districts and residential areas will become another vast challenge to coastal communities and to governments at every level (Heberger *et al.* 2009).

Estimates of how much regional and global sea levels will rise over particular periods of time have been vigorously discussed since the IPCC AR4 estimated a rise of only 18–59 centimetres (cm) over the 21st century. The discussions focus on the dynamic ice changes that were excluded from AR4 estimates because no consensus could be reached based on published literature available at that time (Solomon *et al.* 2009). Since the

Figure 3.4: West Antarctic Ice Sheet vulnerability to collapse

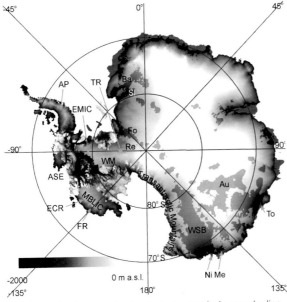

West Antarctic above-sea level surface topography in grey shading and below-sea level topography in browns defining the areas subject to rapid ice collapse. The browns range from 0 to 2000 metres below sea level. For clarity, the ice shelves in West Antarctica are not shown. In East Antarctica, areas more than 200 metres below sea level are indicated by blue shading. *Source: Bamber et al. 2009*

publication of the IPCC AR4, climatological modelling, without dynamic effects explicitly included, suggests that 21st century sea level could rise to 0.5 to 1.4 metres above the 1990 level (Horton *et al.* 2008, Rahmstorf *et al.* 2009). It is clear that while the estimates produced by different modelling studies agree on the general projected trend in global average sea level, they vary in the estimated magnitude of future sea-level rise.

As discussed in the section on Earth's Ice, there are indications of a larger contribution than had been estimated to sea-level rise from dynamic changes of glaciers, ice caps, and the Greenland and West Antarctic Ice Sheets over the last decade. In the shorter term—decades to centuries—glaciers and ice caps may contribute significantly faster to sea level than changes in melt rate alone would indicate. In the longer term—centuries to millennia—the Greenland and West Antarctic Ice Sheets could potentially raise sea level by 6 metres and 3.3 metres, respectively. There is abundant geologic evidence

Figure 3.5: Thermohaline circulation

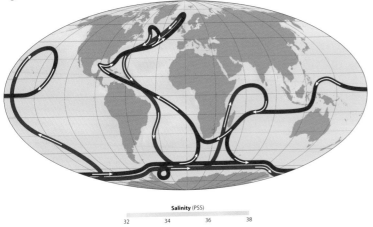

Map shows general location and direction of the warm surface (red) and cold deep-water (blue) currents of the thermohaline circulation. Salinity is represented by colour in units of the Practical Salinity Scale (the conductivity ratio of a sea water sample to a standard KCI solution). Low values (blue) are less saline, while high values (orange) are more saline. *Source: NASA 2005*

that melting ice sheets have raised sea level by very large amounts in decades to centuries, but it is unclear whether this is possible today given the present configurations of bedrock topography and of ice on Greenland and Antarctica (Pfeffer *et al.* 2008, Bamber *et al.* 2009, Dutton *et al.* 2009).

At this time there is still no robust method for modelling future dynamic glacier and ice cap or ice sheet contributions to sea level, but limiting values have been estimated for the next century. By considering rates of discharge from melt and from iceberg fluxes required to drain ice through existing marine outlets, it can be shown that a combined sea-level rise in excess of 1.15 metres from Greenland and Antarctica by 2100 is physically very unlikely. Similarly, glaciers and ice caps are realistically limited to no more than about 0.55 metres by 2100. Introduction of realistic future melt and discharge values into the same analysis suggests that plausible values of total global average sea-level rise, including all land-ice sources plus thermal expansion, may reach 0.8 to 2.0 metres by 2100, although no preferred value was established within this range (Pfeffer *et al.* 2008).

As discussed in Earth Systems (Chapter One), published estimates for sea-level rise beyond 2100 agree that global mean sea levels will continue to rise regardless of changes in the driving forces of ocean thermal expansion and melting of ice (Solomon *et al.* 2009, Siddall *et al.* 2009).

Immediate implications of sea-level rise are already daunting: According to the Institute for Public Works in Australia, for every 20 cm of sea-level rise the frequency of any extreme sea level of a given height increases by a factor of about 10. According to this approach, by 2100, a rise of sea level of 50 cm would produce events every day that now occur once a year and extreme events expected once during the whole of the 20th century will occur several times every year by the end of the 21st century (Hunter 2009). It is obvious that stringent measures will be needed to adapt to sea-level rise.

CIRCULATION

Fresh water from the melting Arctic sea-ice and from the Greenland Ice Sheet enter the North Atlantic and encounter warmer and saltier currents arriving from more temperate latitudes. Changes in quantities and other characteristics of the fresh water could affect dynamics of the thermohaline convection that sink into the deep ocean as a distinct mass and are a driving force of circulation patterns in the Atlantic Ocean.

The deep mixing of ocean waters at high latitudes is important for the heat and carbon uptake of the oceans. This overturning is usually triggered by strong heat loss during the winter season. But with expectations of warming surface waters and the increased influx of fresh water in the high latitudes from sea-ice and glacier melt, it has been suggested that deep mixing may diminish or perhaps even cease in the near future: Both effects, warming and freshening, make the top layer of water less dense and therefore increasingly resistant to deep mixing (Lozier 2009).

As water is removed from the surface, it carries not only heat and salinity anomalies to great depths, but also anthropogenic carbon dioxide, absorbed when the water was still at the surface. The carbon dioxide concentration, like other water-mass properties, is transported to the deep ocean where it remains for hundreds of years. Therefore, the amount of carbon dioxide that has been—and will be—stored in the deep ocean is critically linked to the production of water masses through deep overturning events (Sabine *et al.* 2004).

The vertical exchange that feeds the North Atlantic Deep Water current moving south along the ocean floor seemed to slow for a few years in the early 21st century (Bryden *et al.* 2005, Alley 2007, Lozier 2009). More recently, strong ocean convection in gyres of the sub-polar North Atlantic seems to have returned (Våge *et al.* 2009, Yashayaev and Loder 2009).

The strong mixing documented in the Irminger Sea to the east of Greenland's southern tip and in the Labrador Sea to the southwest is attributed to

Figure 3.6: Deep convection in the subpolar ocean

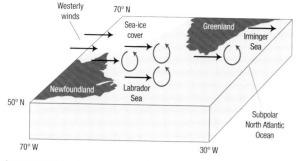

An extensive sea-ice cover maintained the strong, cold, westerly winds until they reached warmer open waters in the central basin of the Labrador Sea and in the Irminger Sea during the winter 2007-2008. There, the unusually cold winds rapidly cooled the surface water, leading to mixing of the water column to depths that had not been reached in the last 15 years. *Source: Lozier 2009*

cold air arriving from Canada that initiates a heat transfer from the ocean to the air, with a consequential sinking mass of cold water. In recent winters, higher temperatures of water flowing south through the Davis Strait have warmed the cold air from the west. However, in the winter of 2007 to 2008 after record Arctic sea-ice loss, the surface water flowing south was melt from that loss, colder and fresher than usual, so with the winter it froze quickly over the Davis Strait. The cold air from the west stayed chilly until it reached the relatively warm water off Greenland, where the subsequent energy exchange triggered renewal of a vertical exchange (Våge *et al.* 2009). This unexpected feedback from colder fresher currents delivered to the west of Greenland demonstrates the complexity of Earth Systems involved in the distribution of heat in a changing climate.

In the Southern Ocean, circulation is closely coupled with the dominant westerly winds that ring Antarctica. Observations show a significant intensification of the Southern Hemisphere westerlies, the prevailing winds between the latitudes of 30° and 60° S, over the past decades. The response of the Antarctic Circumpolar Current and the carbon sink in the Southern Ocean to changes in wind stress and surface buoyancy fluxes is under debate: Do enhanced winds support more upwelling or are they dissipated at levels near the surface? Analysis of data from the Argo network of profiling floats and historical oceanographic records detected coherent hemispheric-scale warming and freshening trends that extend to depths of more than 1,000 metres. The warming and freshening is partly related to changes in the properties of the water masses that make up the Antarctic Circumpolar Current, which are consistent with the anthropogenic changes in heat and freshwater fluxes suggested by climate models (Böning *et al.* 2008).

Beyond meridional overturning and creation of deep water, ocean water from different depths mixes through upwelling processes. Southern Ocean upwelling not only mixes water of differing salinity and temperature but it brings carbon-rich deeper water to the surface and delivers CO_2 to the atmosphere. Upwelling may have been a major contributor to the increase in atmospheric carbon during Pleistocene deglaciation (Anderson *et al.* 2009).

However, absorption of CO_2 by the oceans accounts for 30 to 40 per cent of the excess that has been emitted from anthropogenic sources since the beginning of the industrial revolution (Canadell *et al.* 2007). Recent research has reported a possible slowing in the uptake of CO_2 by the Southern Ocean (Le Quéré *et al.* 2007, Lenton *et al.* 2009).

ACIDIFICATION

Further physical changes in the world's oceans can be attributed to mounting concentrations of CO_2 in the atmosphere. While increases in water temperature and fluctuations between fresh and saline water affect circulation at the surface and with vertical exchange, the repercussions from increasing concentrations of CO_2 in the oceans introduce a separate but

related threat. The ocean's role in absorbing anthropogenic CO_2 released into the atmosphere has been underway for over two centuries. This has altered the chemistry of the global ocean fundamentally, by acidifying the top 2,000 metre layer of the oceans' waters and thus shrinking the total amount of ocean habitat where organisms that incorporate calcium carbonate ($CaCO_3$) into their shells and skeletons can thrive (Caldeira and Wickett 2003, Sabine *et al.* 2004, Orr *et al.* 2005, Denman *et al.* 2007, Feely *et al.* 2008, Ilyina *et al.* 2009, Silverman *et al.* 2009).

Figure 3.7: Aragonite saturation and ocean pH change

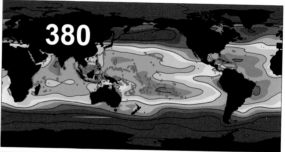

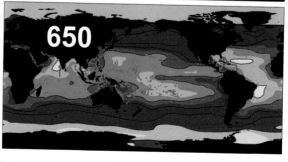

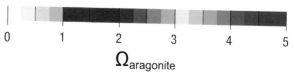

$$\Omega_{aragonite}$$

Changes in surface ocean pH relative to pre-industrial values for different atmospheric CO_2 stabilization levels, 380 ppm and 650 ppm plotted over existing shallow-water coral reef locations (shown as magenta dots). Results are obtained by adding model-predicted perturbations in geochemical fields to modern observations, except for the Arctic Ocean where results are model simulations only due to a lack of observations. *Source: Cao and Caldeira 2008*

Box 3.2 The chemistry of acidification

The oceanic uptake of anthropogenic CO_2 occurs through a series of well-known chemical reactions that increase aqueous CO_2, lower seawater pH, and lower carbonate ion levels. To the beginning of the 21st century, anthropogenic CO_2 has reduced average surface ocean acidity to 8.1 pH units from a pre-industrial value of 8.2 pH units on a logarithmic scale, a 30 per cent increase in acidity (Caldeira and Wickett 2003, Caldeira 2009). Acidification decreases the concentration of carbonate (CO_3), decreasing the saturation state of the $CaCO_3$ mineral calcite in the upper ocean that many marine organisms need to metabolize the shells and skeletons that support their functions.

Projected increase in anthropogenic CO_2 emissions will accelerate these chemical changes to rates unprecedented in the recent geological record. At current emission rates, atmospheric CO_2 concentrations will increase from 385 parts per million (ppm) in 2008 to 450–650 ppm by 2060, which would decrease average ocean surface acidity to an average of 7.9–7.8 pH units and reduce the saturation states of calcite and aragonite, two more $CaCO_3$ minerals, by 25 per cent—further shrinking optimal regions for biological carbonate formation (Doney and Schimel 2007, Doney et al. 2009, Steinacher et al. 2009, Cooley and Doney 2009).

Seasonal acidification events are already appearing—water that can corrode aragonite is welling up during the summer months along the California coastline, decades earlier than models predict (Feely et al. 2008). Researchers are anticipating the same degree of corrosive water in some high-latitude polar and subpolar locations by 2050 or earlier (Steinacher et al. 2009). But these model predictions and logical anticipations may be too conservative because they are based on scenarios that expected some decrease in CO_2 emissions by the early 21st century. Estimated fossil-fuel CO_2 emissions in 2005 exceeded those predicted by the most extreme scenario from the 1990s implying that future atmospheric CO_2 levels may exceed current model predictions, and the oceans may acidify faster than presently forecast.

Ongoing ocean acidification may harm a wide range of marine organisms and the food webs that depend on them, eventually degrading entire marine ecosystems (Fabry et al. 2008, Silverman et al. 2009, Doney et al. 2009). Laboratory studies suggest that molluscs, including species that support valuable marine fisheries such as mussels and oysters, and especially their juveniles, are particularly sensitive to these changes (Gazeau et al. 2007, Kurihara et al. 2007, Kurihara et al. 2009, Cooley and Doney 2009).

Figure 3.8: How ocean acidification works

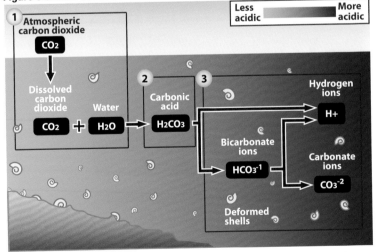

1. Up to one half of the carbon dioxide (CO_2) released by burning fossil fuels over the past 200 years has been absorbed by the world's oceans
2. Absorbed CO_2 in seawater (H_2O) forms carbonic acid (H_2CO_3), lowering the water's pH level and making it more acidic
3. This raises the hydrogen ion concentration in the water, and limits organisms' access to carbonate ions, which are needed to form hard outer shells

Source: Adapted from University of Maryland 2009

Organisms' net responses to rising CO_2 will vary, depending on sensitivities to decreasing seawater pH, carbonate concentration, and carbonate saturation state and to increasing oceanic total inorganic carbon and gaseous CO_2. Shell-forming marine organisms create carbonate structures using one of two approaches:

Organisms that exert low biological control over calcification directly deposit $CaCO_3$ along their inner shell walls. Consequently, they depend on a sufficient ambient carbonate concentration to accumulate shells successfully. Commercially valuable molluscs such as scallops and oysters and some gastropods such as conchs use this method to build shells. Shells deposited in this manner are more likely to contain aragonite, a more soluble mineral form of $CaCO_3$. Corals form aragonite skeletons around their exterior, while coralline algae secrete aragonite or magnesium calcite, a moderately soluble form of $CaCO_3$ (Fabry et al. 2008, Doney et al. 2009).

Organisms that exert high biological control over calcification typically accumulate intracellular stocks of carbonate ions, gradually hardening their chitin and protein exoskeletons from within by depositing $CaCO_3$, the least soluble form of calcite. Sea urchins and crustaceans, including lobsters, shrimp, and crabs, follow this model and therefore do not require specific seawater chemistry to form shells. An organism's ultimate responses will also depend on factors such as individual history or genetic variability (Doney et al. 2009).

Many organisms, some of which are commercially valuable, also exhibit a range of damages to functions such as metabolism, reproduction, development, and immunity (Fabry et al. 2008, Holman et al. 2004, Burgents et al. 2005). Still unknown are the effects of acidification on the ability of fish to grow internal carbonate structures, which are important because they determine their advantages for feeding and migration.

However, crabs, lobsters, shrimp, some planktons, and other organisms increase calcification or photosynthesis in seawater that is high in CO_2 (Ries et al. 2008a, Ries et al. 2008b, Doney et al. 2009). Whether the observed cases of increased calcification or photosynthesis result in any kind of advantage is not known. However, decreases in calcification and biological function due to ocean acidification are capable of decreasing the fitness of commercially valuable groups by directly damaging shells or by compromising early development and survival (Kurihara et al. 2007, Kurihara et al. 2009, Gazeau et al. 2007).

Ocean acidification's total effects on the marine environment will depend also on ecosystem responses. Even if carbonate-forming organisms do form shells and skeletons in elevated CO_2 conditions, they may encounter high energy costs that could reduce survival and reproduction (Wood et al. 2008, Kleypas et al. 2006). Losses of plankton, juvenile shellfish, and other organisms at the bottom of marine food chains have the potential to reduce harvests of economically important predator species. At the same time, acidic conditions will damage coral and prevent its re-growth, destroying crucial marine 'nursery' habitats and disrupting feeding and reproduction processes in a range of species (Kleypas et al. 2006, Lumsden et al. 2007).

Ecological shifts to algal overgrowth and decreased species diversity sometimes follow after coral disturbances, creating new ecosystem states that are stable but are then dominated by herbivores and less commercially valuable species. Ocean acidification has been implicated in similar ecological shifts from corals and other calcifying organisms to sea grasses and algae in communities with decreasing pH (Norström et al. 2009, Hall-Spencer et al. 2008, Wootton et al. 2009, Scheffer et al. 2001, Hoegh-Guldberg et al. 2007).

Ocean acidification will affect coral reefs and the ecosystems that depend on them in the more temperate latitudes because the processes involved are more robust in colder water. Coral reefs in warmer waters are subjected to the threat of coral bleaching.

Figure 3.9: Distribution of coldwater and tropical coral reefs

Coral reefs

■ Warm water   ■ Cold water

The coldwater reefs are highly susceptible to ocean acidification from climate change, which has its greatest impacts at high latitudes, while tropical reefs will become severely damaged by rising sea temperatures. In addition, both reef types must adapt to sea-level rise. *Source: UNEP 2008b*

CUMULATIVE EFFECTS

Since the early 1980s, episodes of coral reef bleaching and mortality, due primarily to climate-induced ocean warming, have occurred almost annually in one or more of the world's tropical or subtropical seas. Bleaching is episodic, with the most severe events typically accompanying coupled ocean–atmosphere phenomena, such as the El Niño Southern Oscillation, which result in sustained regional elevations of ocean temperature. Bleaching episodes have resulted in catastrophic loss of coral cover in some locations, and have changed coral community structure in many others, with a potentially critical influence on the maintenance of biodiversity in the marine tropics (Donner *et al.* 2007).

Bleaching has also set the stage for other declines in reef health, such as increases in coral diseases, the breakdown of reef framework by bioeroders, and the loss of critical habitat for associated reef fishes and other biota. Secondary ecological effects, such as the concentration of predators on remnant surviving coral populations, have also accelerated the pace of decline in some areas. Although bleaching severity and recovery have been variable across all spatial scales, some reefs have experienced relatively rapid recovery from severe bleaching impacts. Bleaching disturbances are likely to become a chronic stress in many reef areas in the coming decades, but if coral communities were exposed to the stress less intensely and over longer periods of time, they could adapt to changing conditions (Donner *et al.* 2007). Some reefs degraded by multiple stressors may already be approaching their end, although to date there has not been any global extinction of individual coral species as a result of bleaching events (Baker *et al.* 2008). Should such bleaching events increase in intensity and frequency, as has been projected by the best models, they will seriously degrade these important ecosystems.

If coral reefs were only threatened by rising sea levels they could possibly grow at the accelerated rates that are likely for the next century at least. But acidification and warming, as well as pollution and physical destruction, are weakening reefs further and they are unlikely to continue to provide 'fish nursery services' at the optimal rates required for healthy marine ecosystems (Hoegh-Guldberg *et al.* 2009).

Box 3.3 The Coral Triangle

Coral bleaching results when colonies of colorful photosynthesizing zooxanthellae algae abandon the calcareous structures built by coral polyps. Once bleached, the structures may or may not be re-colonized to re-establish the symbiotic relationships that characterize healthy reefs. Over the last three decades, coral reefs have experienced severe mass bleaching events in many tropical regions, including the Coral Triangle that stretches across six countries of Southeast Asia and Melanesia.

A recent review of coral reef health in the Coral Triangle indicates that acidification, warmer temperatures, and rising sea levels have already damaged coastal ecosystems. These three climate change-related processes act as stresses in addition to other anthropogenic threats such as destructive and unsustainable fishing techniques, increased chemical pollution, and higher levels of sedimentation due to onshore land use practices.

Source: Baskett et al. 2009, Hoegh-Guldberg et al. 2009, Oliver and Palumbi 2009

EARTH'S ECOSYSTEMS

Earth's Ecosystems

Since the compilation of the IPCC's Fourth Assessment Report, serious and irreversible changes in Earth's Ecosystems due to anthropogenic activities are increasingly recognized with greater confidence and better quantification of the processes.

Mau Complex, the largest closed-canopy forest in Kenya, is under severe threat from land use change and could suffer further degradation from a changing climate. *Source: A. Kirk*

For both marine and terrestrial ecosystems, the most challenging irreversible climate-related changes include altered chemical characteristics of the ambient environment, inundation of many small-islands and low-lying coastal ecosystems by sea-level rise, loss of wetland quantity and quality, and increased aridity in subtropical areas. These expected irreversible changes and their cumulative effects, proceeding at unprecedented rates, will alter ecosystem characteristics resulting in potential species extinction.

Local and subnational research into ongoing climate-related ecosystem changes is proliferating in countries and regions that support active investigative science programmes. The understanding gained from these efforts could provide analogues for changes in less well-documented regions. Only a sampling of new research can be addressed in this Compendium and hopefully their worth as potential analogues will be eventually proven.

Documenting the effects of climate change on ecosystems at global scales has consistently challenged the IPCC, mainly because of the scarcity of peer-reviewed research findings from Latin America, Africa, and Asia (McCarthy *et al.* 2001, Rosenzweig *et al.* 2008). However, since the closing date for submissions to the IPCC's Fourth Assessment Report (AR4), wide-ranging surveys have been conducted and analysis suggests that ecological changes in the phenology and distribution of plants and animals are occurring in all well-studied marine, freshwater, and terrestrial groups (Parmesan 2006). Range-restricted species, particularly polar and mountaintop species, show severe range contractions and have been the first groups in which species have gone extinct due to recent climate change. Tropical coral reefs and amphibians have been most negatively affected. Predator-prey and plant-insect interactions have been disrupted when interacting species have responded differently to warming (Parmesan 2006).

A comprehensive 2008 analysis of more than 29,000 data series from all continents, some covering over 35 years of observations, verifies these findings and goes further by attributing such changes to anthropogenic climate change (Rosenzweig *et al.* 2008). In marine ecosystems these responses include shifts from cold-adapted to warm-adapted communities,

phenological changes, and alterations in species' interactions. In terrestrial ecosystems, responses include shifts to earlier onset of spring events such as leaf unfolding, blooming date, migration, and reproduction timing; change in species distribution; and modification of community structure. Contributing changes in physical systems include shrinking glaciers, melting permafrost, coastal erosion, shifts in river discharge peaks, and warming in lakes and rivers with effects on stratification and chemistry (Rosenzweig *et al.* 2008).

The 2008 analysis explicitly considered the influence of land-use change, management practices, pollution, and human demographic shifts as drivers of the observed environmental changes and was able to eliminate the affected data series from their review (Rosenzweig *et al.* 2008). This broad consideration strengthens the robustness of the findings and offers a model for future analyses. The approach has stimulated further documentation and synthesis in recent months (Lyon *et al.* 2008, Pörtner and Farrell 2008, Hegland *et al.* 2008, Chazal and Rounsevell 2009, Lawler *et al.* 2009, Cheung *et al.* 2009, Füssel 2009).

MARINE ECOSYSTEMS

The effects of climate variability on marine life have been under observation for decades. Thus the empirical evidence, and the theory that frames it, indicate that environmental conditions in the oceans including temperature, acidity, currents, and productivity are continuing to exhibit signs of change (Cheung *et al.* 2008, Rahel and Olden 2008, Dulvy *et al.* 2008, Beaugrand *et al.* 2009). Marine biodiversity, however, remains poorly understood and scarcely studied at the global scale: The influence of human impact on marine ecosystems has only been recently mapped at a global scale using standardized categories of effects (Halpern *et al.* 2008). Only a very limited number of studies have attempted to investigate the impacts of climate change on species richness, community assemblages, and distributions of biodiversity at the ocean basin or global scales. Previous research has focused on specific regions and particular ranges of taxa (Rosenzweig *et al.* 2008, Jackson 2008, Miles 2009).

Researchers are now able to project global patterns of invasion, extinction, and the combined effect of species turnover to the year 2050 using a recently developed dynamic climate envelope model (Cheung *et al.* 2009). The study plotted future distributional ranges of 1,066 economically valuable marine fish and invertebrate species. The results suggest that the global scale and pattern of consequences for marine biodiversity from climate changes are consistent with those found for terrestrial ecosystems. By 2050, ecosystems in subpolar regions, the tropics, and semi-enclosed seas will have undergone numerous local extinctions. Conversely, the Arctic and Southern Oceans will experience severe species invasions. The impacts of climate change on marine biodiversity may result in a dramatic species turnover of up to 60 per cent in this first quantitative estimation of marine biodiversity impacts at the global scale (Cheung *et al.* 2009).

In the face of such challenges, the cumulative effects of higher temperatures, changes in ocean circulation, and ocean acidification are under serious examination (Jackson 2008, Miles 2009). Additional variables involving oxygen and nitrogen levels are also being incorporated into models and analyses

Table 4.1: Marine ecosystem disturbance

	Symptoms	Drivers
Coral reefs	—Live coral reduced 50-93 per cent; fish populations reduced 90 per cent —Apex predators virtually absent; other megafauna reduced by 90-100 per cent —Population explosions of sea-weeds; loss of complex habitat —Mass mortality of corals from disease and coral bleaching	—Overfishing —Warming and acidifica-tion due to increasing CO_2 —Runoff of nutrients and toxins —Invasive species
Estuar-ies and coastal seas	—Marshlands, mangroves, seagrasses, and oyster reefs reduced 67-91 per cent —Fish and other shellfish popula-tions reduced 50-80 per cent —Eutrophication and hypoxia, sometimes of entire estuaries, with mass mortality of fishes and invertebrates —Loss of native species —Toxic algal blooms —Outbreaks of disease —Contamination and infection of fish and shellfish, human disease	—Overfishing —Runoff of nutrients and toxins —Warming due to rise of CO_2 —Invasive species —Coastal land use
Conti-nental shelves	—Loss of complex benthic habitat, fishes and sharks reduced 50-99 per cent —Eutrophication and hypoxia in 'dead zones' near river mouths —Toxic algal blooms —Contamination and infection of fish and shellfish —Decreased upwelling of nutrients —Changes in plankton communities	—Overfishing —Trophic cascades —Trawling —Runoff of nutrients and toxins —Warming and acidifica-tion due to increasing CO_2 —Species —Escape of aquaculture species
Open ocean pelagic	—Commercially targeted fishes reduced 50-90 per cent —Increase in nontargeted fish —Increased stratification —Changes in plankton communities	—Overfishing

Status and trends of major ocean ecosystems defined by principal symptoms and drivers of degradation in more than 99 per cent of the global ocean that is unprotected from exploitation. *Source: Jackson 2008*

(Kwon *et al.* 2009, Scheffer *et al.* 2009, Voss and Montoya 2009, Ward *et al.* 2009). The implications of these cumulative effects and of chemical cycle responses have profound significance for marine species and for the harvests that humans expect to reap through the 21st century (Schubert *et al.* 2006, Jackson 2008, Brewer and Peltzer 2009, Doney *et al.* 2009).

Ocean acidification

Preliminary findings from the field are verifying results from laboratory experiments, and scientific understanding of ocean acidification's ef-fects on the marine species and ecosystems is underway (see Earth's Oceans, Chapter Three). Initial concerns over ocean acidification focused on reduced calcification in coral reefs and other calcareous organisms, but other concerns are emerging. Elevated dissolved CO_2 concentrations may impose a physiological strain on marine animals, impairing perform-ance and requiring energy that would otherwise be used for locomotion, predation, reproduction, or coping with other environmental stresses such as warming oceans (Guinotte *et al.* 2008, Brewer and Peltzer 2009). However, long-term progress and consequences of changing seawater chemistry on marine ecosystems and their various member species can only be theorized. Some data sets have allowed an identification of ocean chemistry thresholds when acidification will cause net carbonate

Figure 4.1: Modelled ocean acidification

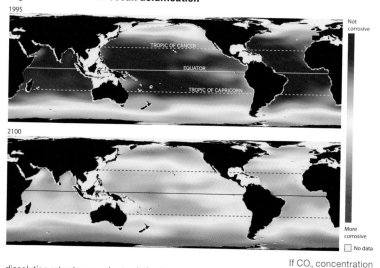

If CO_2 concentration continues to rise un-checked, models show that acidification will deplete carbonate ions in much of the global ocean by 2100, turning the waters corrosive for many shell-building ani-mals. *Source: National Geographic 2007*

dissolution rates to exceed net calcification rates in whole coral reef systems (Hoegh-Guldberg *et al.* 2007).

The degree to which ocean acidification influences critical physi-ological or ontogenetic processes is essential knowledge for the proper response: These processes are important drivers of calcifica-tion, ecosystem structure and function, biodiversity, and ultimately ecosystem health. Research into the synergistic effects of ocean acidification and other human-induced environmental changes on marine food webs and the potential transformative effects these changes could have on marine ecosystems is urgently needed (Guinotte *et al.* 2008).

Some success has been seen through establishment and enforcement of marine protected areas (MPA) in efforts to encourage growth of fish populations (UNEP 2008b, UNEP 2009). Climate change represents a new and serious threat to marine ecosystems, but, to date, few studies have specifically considered how to design MPA networks to be resilient to this emerging threat. Researchers have compiled the best available information on MPA network design and supplemented it with specific recommendations for building resilience into these networks to help MPA planners and managers design MPA networks that are more robust in the face of climate change impacts (MacLeod *et al.* 2008).

Coastal processes

Ecological studies often focus on average effects of environmental fac-tors, but ecological dynamics and ecosystem functioning may depend as much or more upon environmental extremes and variability, especially in coastal regions where extreme events are expected to increase in

Figure 4.2: Location of Marine Protected Areas around the world

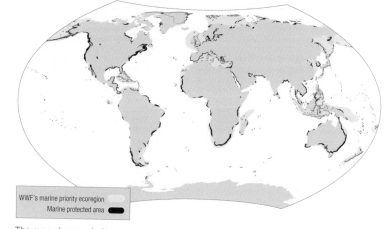

The map shows priority ecoregions as well as the global distribution of Marine Protected Areas in 2005. *Source: WWF 2005*

Figure 4.3: Irrawaddy River Delta washes away

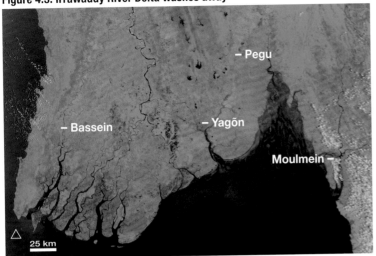

Satellite images of the Myanmar coast on 15 April 2008 (top) before Cyclone Nargis and 5 May 2008 (bottom) after Nargis hit the region, showing the devastation of flooding over the coastal area. *Source: UNEP 2009, NASA 2008*

and capacity of coastal and inland forest ecosystems to deliver ecosystem services such as carbon sequestration, storm protection, pollution control, habitat support, and food production. The evaluation is considering coastal wetland and inland forest sites across the US representing continental-level gradients of precipitation, temperature, vegetation, frequency of occurrence of major windstorms, tidal range, watershed land use, and sediment availability. Once the methodologies are established, similar networks could be created in other regions to evaluate the implications of sea-level rise and windstorm effects at local and subnational scales (Hopkinson *et al.* 2008).

Physiological and biogeochemical responses of terrestrial ecosystems are determined by prevailing ecological and meteorological conditions. However, sudden extreme events can provoke the crossing of mortality thresholds for certain organisms and trigger population decline, decrease resilience, and alter community and ecosystem structure over time (Fagre *et al.* 2009, Running and Mills 2009).

Another less appreciated but critical determinant of terrestrial ecosystem structure and functioning, particularly as it relates to life-cycle timing of seasonal plant phenology and plant growth responses, is the amplification of variability in climate and environmental conditions (Post *et al.* 2008, Fagre *et al.* 2009, Running and Mills 2009). Amplification in natural variability intensities due to climate change introduces a new urgency for understanding the biological consequences of environmental extremes (Knapp *et al.* 2008).

Recent work on changes in, and predictability of, return times demonstrate that the coincidence of otherwise normal events can lead to environmental extremes. Using techniques based on paleontological species-resilience models, researchers are developing methods to measure disturbance from extreme events and their effects on species throughout particular ecosystems. Further efforts will focus on distinguishing between events resulting from coincidence of background variabilities and new stresses introduced by climate change (Denny *et al.* 2009).

Mangroves

Mangrove forests, those vast twisted habitats found in tidal zones along many tropical and subtropical coastlines, provide aquatic feeding grounds and nurseries for fish. In addition to their crucial and well-documented role in estuarine and coastal fishery food chains, mangrove forests have recently been found to provide important protection and stabilization services for low-lying coastal lands (Thampanya *et al.* 2006, Bosire *et al.* 2008, Kairo *et al.* 2008).

A number of studies have suggested that the resilience of mangrove ecosystems can be observed in their recovery patterns following severe natural disturbance. Mangroves have demonstrated considerable resilience over timescales proportional to shoreline evolution, demonstrated by current soil accretion rates in mangrove forests that are effectively keeping pace with average sea-level rise (Alongi 2008).

Despite their tremendous ecological value, mangroves suffer one of the fastest degradation rates of any global habitat—exceeding 1 per cent of total mangrove area per year (Kairo *et al.* 2008). Roughly half the world's mangrove area has already been lost since the beginning of the 20th century. The major causes for this decline include overexploitation, harvesting, pollution, and shrimp farming. About 35 per cent of that mangrove loss has occurred since 1990—and 25 per cent of that total is from shrimp farms (Gilman *et al.* 2006, Thampanya *et al.* 2006, Bosire *et al.* 2008).

Mangroves might be able to adapt to rising sea levels and continue to protect coasts from storm surges, to filter sediments, and to shelter fish larvae and fingerlings. But, with the build-up of human settlements and other infrastructure in coastal zones, there is no place to which mangroves can retreat (Alongi 2008, MacLeod and Salm 2006). The consequences of losing these critical coastal ecosystems on marine biology, and ultimately

intensity and frequency. Theoretically, as ocean surface and atmospheric temperatures warm, the hydrologic cycle will speed up—more moisture will evaporate from oceans and lakes, and plants and soils will give up more water through transpiration and evaporation because warmer air is capable of holding more water vapour. Also, as oceans warm, they should have more energy to supply tropical cyclonic winds. Sporadic observations over the long-term and changing data analysis abilities render varying conclusions. Some analyses have detected little change in frequency and intensity of cyclones globally during the last 20 years, while other evidence shows that the strongest cyclones have become more intense in all storm-prone regions (Klotzbach 2006, Elsner *et al.* 2008).

However, models and observations agree that sudden downpours will become more common in some regions, leading to more frequent flooding and associated soil erosion and slope collapse. In fact, observed increases in rainfall are greater than the models have predicted, implying that the expected intensity of rainfall may have been underestimated (Allan and Soden 2008).

In addition, human populations and the ecosystems that supply them with food, fibre, water, building material, and other resources are still threatened by the storms that will penetrate further inland with rising sea levels (Aumann *et al.* 2008). Storm surges, such as the one delivered by Cyclone Nargis to the Irrawaddy Delta, can contaminate coastal fields with saltwater at the surface while sea-level rise can result in saltwater incursions in freshwater aquifers that supply groundwater resources (UNEP 2009).

Researchers are evaluating how two aspects of climate change, sea-level rise and intensification of windstorms, will influence the structure, function,

on human beings, are enormous (Hoegh-Guldberg *et al.* 2009, Brown 2007, Alongi 2008, Chatenoux and Peduzzi 2007, UNEP-WCMC 2006, Vermaat and Thampanya 2007, Brown 2007).

Along many lowland sea coasts, tidal marshes provide significant levels of productivity but the threat from ongoing sea-level rise is not well understood. Study of tidal marshes at the lower and upper salinity ranges, and their attendant delivery of ecosystem services, will be most affected by accelerated sea-level rise, unless human demographic and topographic conditions enable tidal freshwater marshes to migrate inland, or unless vertical accretion of salt marshes increases as it does in mangroves, to compensate for accelerated sea-level rise (Craft *et al.* 2009).

Islands

Sea-level rise presents an imminent threat to freshwater-dependent ecosystems on small oceanic islands, which often harbour rare and endemic species. Once sea level reaches a critical threshold, the transition from a landscape characterized by dryland forests and freshwater wetlands to one dominated by sea grasses and mangroves can occur suddenly, following a single storm-surge event. Efforts to manage species' survival and to support conditions that form refuges for threatened ecosystems are currently under development with the goal of serving as models for species-rich coastal ecosystems under threat globally (Ross *et al.* 2008).

Saltwater contamination is particularly difficult to handle on small islands because there is little possibility to retreat to available land at higher levels. Together with shore erosion, saltwater incursions into agricultural areas are already driving island populations from their communities (UN 2008).

TERRESTRIAL ECOSYSTEMS

As has been presented, climate change affects a wide range of components of the Earth's systems. Individual components of the systems react with a wide range of response times at different scales to increasing GHG concentrations in the atmosphere. While radiative forcing changes almost instantaneously as atmospheric GHG levels rise, warming of surface air temperatures, melting of ice sheets, and sea-level rise will continue long after atmospheric GHG levels have been stabilized. These long-term changes are referred to as the 'climate change commitment': Conditions that we have already committed to because of earlier actions—or inactions. The concept of unavoidable commitments has so far mostly applied to physical properties of the climate system. However, the concept can be extended to terrestrial ecosystems (Jones *et al.* 2009, Plattner 2009).

The global terrestrial biosphere shows significant inertia in its response to climate change. As well, it will continue to change for decades after climate stabilization (Brovkin *et al.* 2009). Ecosystems can be committed to long-term change long before any response is observable: For example, the risk of significant loss of forest cover in Amazonia rises rapidly for a global mean temperature rise of about 2 degrees Celsius. Such unavoidable ecosystem changes must be considered in the definition of dangerous climate change (Jones *et al.* 2009).

Increases in temperature over the last century have clearly been linked to shifts in species' distributions. Given the magnitude of projected future climatic changes, even larger range shifts can be expected for the 21st century. These changes will, in turn, alter ecological communities and the functioning of ecosystems. Uncertainties in climate change projections at local and sub-national scales make it difficult for conservation managers and planners to proactively adapt to climate stresses (Post *et al.* 2008, Seastedt *et al.* 2008, UNEP 2009).

One study addressed this uncertainty by assessing the potential effects of expected changes on the geographic ranges of about 3,000 Western Hemisphere species of amphibians, birds, and mammals using 30 future climate simulations with coupled atmosphere–ocean general circulation models. Eighty per cent of the climate projections based on a relatively low

Figure 4.4: Sundarbans Protected Area

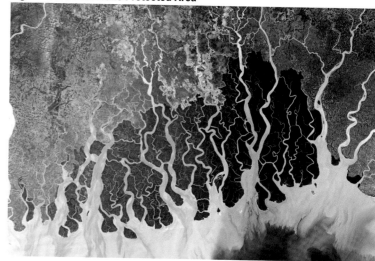

greenhouse-gas emissions scenario resulted in the local loss of at least 10 per cent of the vertebrate fauna over much of North and South America. The largest changes in fauna are predicted for the tundra, Central America, and the Andes Mountains where certain areas are likely to experience over 90 per cent species change, so that future faunal assemblages, diversities, and distributions will bear little resemblance to those of today (Lawler *et al.* 2009).

Disappearing and novel climates

The loss of whole, or even parts of, faunal assemblages entails the disappearance of species and ecosystems—and the evolution of new ones. Based upon an appreciation of paleobiogeographical principles, researchers suggest that the concept of disappearing and novel climates might be useful for understanding the changes that are expected over the next century and more (Williams *et al.* 2007, MacDonald *et al.* 2008, Seastedt *et al.* 2008).

Climate is a primary control on species distributions and ecosystem processes, so novel 21st century climates may promote formation of novel species associations and other ecological surprises, whereas the disappearance of some extant climates certainly threatens extinction for species through loss of habitat and of ecosystem integrity. Novel climates are projected to develop primarily in the tropics and subtropics, whereas disappearing climates are concentrated in tropical montane regions and the poleward portions of continents.

This satellite image shows mangrove forest in the Sundarbans protected area. The mangroves appear deep green, surrounded to the north by a landscape of agricultural lands, which appear lighter green; and by towns, which appear tan; and by streams, which appear blue. *Source: NASA 2006b*

New Caledonia is one of many small island developing states that are vulnerable to climate change. *Source: L.G. Roger/Stillpictures*

Table 4.2: Interlinkages among climate changes, plant and animal response, and economic activity

Effects on Species		Phenology – spring arrival – autumn arrival – growing season length	Temperature – means – extremes – variability – seasonality	Rainfall – means – extremes – variability – seasonality	Extreme events – storms – floods – droughts – fires	CO₂ concentrations – atmospheric – ocean – ocean pH
Changes in competitive ability	[Fisheries]		●			●
Uncoupling of mutualisms (including pollinator loss and coral bleaching)	[Agriculture] [Fisheries]	●	●	●		
Changes in fecundity leading to changing population structure	[Agriculture] [Fisheries] [Animal husbandry]		●	●	●	
Uncoupling of parasite-host relationships	[Human health] [Agriculture]	●	●			
Inability to form calcareous structures and dissolving of aragonite	[Fisheries]					●
Change in distribution ranges	[Agriculture] [Fisheries]		●	●	●	
Desynchronization of migration of dispersal events	[Agriculture] [Fisheries]	●	●	●		
Increased physiological stress causing direct mortality and increased disease suspectibility	[Human health] [Animal husbandry] [Fisheries]		●	●	●	●
Uncoupling of predator-prey relationships	[Animal husbandry] [Fisheries]	●	●	●		
Changes in sex ratio	[Agriculture] [Fisheries] [Animal husbandry]		●	●		
Loss in habitat	[Animal husbandry] [Fisheries]		●	●	●	
Interactions with new pathogens and invasives	[Agriculture] [Fisheries] [Human health]	●	●	●		

Legend: Agriculture · Animal husbandry · Fisheries · Human health

The changing climate is affecting the timing and quantity of water availability, the length of growing seasons, and the life cycles of pests and pathogens. These in turn put pressure on various species of plants and animals, with ultimate consequences for a variety of economic and development activities. *Source: Foden et al. 2008*

Under the highest IPCC emissions scenario—the one that most closely matches current trends—12–39 per cent of the planet's terrestrial surface could experience novel climate conditions and 10–48 per cent could suffer disappearing climates by the end of this century. Dispersal limitations—imposed by fragmented habitats and physical obstructions, including those built by humans—increase the risk that species will experience the loss of existing climates or the emergence of novel climates. There is a close correspondence between regions with globally disappearing climates and previously identified biodiversity hotspots. While most changes are predicted to occur at high latitudes and high altitudes, many tropical species are incapable of tolerating anything beyond mild temperature variations. Even slight warming may threaten them. Ecosystem niche gaps left by migrating species in tropical lowland ecosystems may endanger those species that are able to adapt to changes within an ecosystem at a particular location, but not to the absence of a key player in that ecosystem (Williams *et al.* 2007, Tewksbury *et al.* 2008, Colwell *et al.* 2008).

To address the problems of ecosystem loss in the face of climate change, ecosystem management efforts are increasingly recognizing that many ecosystems are now sufficiently altered in structure and function to qualify as novel systems. Given this assumption, attempts to 'restore' systems to within their historical range of location, characteristics, or processes may not be possible. In such circumstances, management activities directed at removing undesirable features of novel ecosystems may perpetuate or create ecosystems that will not survive. Management actions should attempt to maintain genetic and species diversity while encouraging the biogeochemical characteristics that favour the more desirable species (Seastedt *et al.* 2008).

SHIFTING CLIMATIC ZONES

Changes in the tropics are becoming more apparent. Several lines of evidence show that over the past few decades the tropical belt, which roughly encompasses equatorial regions, is expanding. This influences all latitudinally determined climatologies, including the intertropical convergence zone, the subtropical dry zones, and the westerlies that dominate weather at subpolar latitudes. The observed rate of expansion already exceeds climate model projections for expansion during the 21st century. This expansion of the tropics not only has a cascading effect on large scale circulation systems but also on precipitation patterns that determine natural ecosystems, agricultural productivities, and water resources for urban and industrial demands. Expansion of the hot and humid tropical zone leads to poleward displacement of the subtropical zones, areas occupied by most of the world's deserts (Seidel *et al.* 2008, Lu *et al.* 2009, Seager *et al.* 2007, Johanson and Fu 2009, Sachs *et al.* 2009).

Precipitation changes and dry-season rainfall reduction

In many regions of the world, water is already scarce and, given increased pressures from agriculture and urban expansion, is likely to become more so as global climate change advances. Shortages of water for agriculture and for basic human needs are threatening communities around the world. Southeastern Australia has been short of water for nearly a decade and southwestern North America may have already transitioned to a perennial drought crisis climate (Murphy and Timbal 2008, MacDonald *et al.* 2008).

According to projections, areas expected to be affected by persistent drought and water scarcity in coming years include the southern and northern parts of Africa, the Mediterranean, much of the Middle East, a broad band in Central Asia and the Indian subcontinent, southern and eastern Australia, northern Mexico, and the southwestern United States—a distribution similar to current water-stressed regions (IPCC 2007a, Solomon *et al.* 2009). Regional studies are following up on these projections and others from drought-threatened regions.

Figure 4.5: Novel and disappearing climates

+3.4° C
Novel climates
+1.8° C

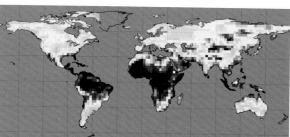
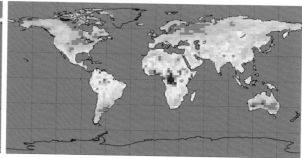

Disappearing climates

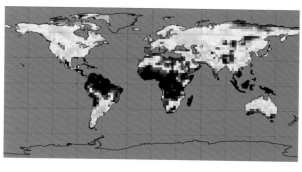
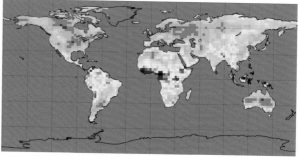

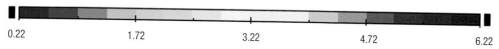

| 0.22 | 1.72 | 3.22 | 4.72 | 6.22 |

World map of disappearing climates and novel climates under two of the IPCC scenarios, one that projects a 3.4° C temperature increase and one that projects an increase of 1.8° C. Changes occur almost everywhere—yellows and reds indicate more change from current conditions, blue indicates less change. *Source: Williams et al. 2007*

Northern Africa

Debate continues about whether the Sahel, one of the world's most vulnerable regions to climate variability, is at a tipping point. Some projections suggest that the Sahel region of West Africa could see a sudden revival of rains if global warming and changes in ocean temperatures in the North Atlantic combine to trigger a strengthening of the West African monsoon. This tipping point has been crossed in the past: Between 9,000 and 5,000 years ago, large parts of the Sahel were verdant after an exceptionally dry period around 10,500 years ago. Evidence published in 2008 suggested that even if this revival occurs it may not be as abrupt as some suggest. A study of pollen and lake sediments in the Sahara investigated how the Sahel went from wet to dry conditions over a 1,000 year period that began 6,000 years ago. Other studies suggest this shift happened within a few decades. The search for a reliable means of predicting future precipitation patterns in the Sahel region of Africa continues, with one study suggesting that links to sea surface temperatures that held in the 20th century might not apply in the 21st century (Kröpelin *et al.* 2008, Brovkin and Claussen 2008, Cook 2008).

Mediterranean

New research confirms that by the end of the 21st century the Mediterranean region will experience more severe increases in aridity than previously estimated. This aridity will render the entire region, particularly the southern Mediterranean, vulnerable to water stress and desertification. Using the highest resolution projections published for the entire Mediterranean basin, researchers project a substantial northward expansion of dry and semi-arid regime lands across the Iberian, Italian, Hellenic, and Turkish peninsulas. These results imply a corresponding retreat of temperate oceanic and continental climate regimes and a likely shift in vegetation cover, with huge implications for agriculture in the region. This

study adds to the body of work that corresponds to and projects from the region's ongoing observations of warming and drying trends (Iglesias *et al.* 2007, Diffenbaugh *et al.* 2007, Gao and Giorgi 2008, Lionello *et al.* 2008).

Southwestern North America

In the southwestern region of North America, modelled trajectories toward intensified aridity in the 21st century and a sustained drier climate in the region are consistent with observed patterns. Researchers suggest that a transition to a more arid climate in the southwestern US is already underway, perhaps since 2000. It will likely be only a matter of years before drought becomes the region's new climatology. Unlike the multi-year droughts of 1950s western North America—attributed to variations in sea surface temperatures or El Niño Southern Oscillation effects—the projected intensified aridity in the Southwest is the result of an increased divergence of large-scale moisture regimes and other changes in atmospheric circulation cells linked to poleward expansion of the subtropical dry zones. The 21st century drying of these subtropical areas in the region is unlike any climate state seen in the instrumental record. The most severe future droughts will still occur during persistent La Niña events, but they will be worse than current extremes because the La Niña conditions will be perturbing a drier base state (Seager *et al.* 2007, Barnett *et al.* 2008, MacDonald *et al.* 2008).

Amazon rainforest

Amazonia faces dual threats from deforestation and from climate change in the 21st century (Malhi *et al.* 2008). While deforestation is the most visible threat to the Amazon ecosystem, climate change is emerging as a creeping threat to the future of the region. Currently, the major agent of change in the Amazon forest ecosystem is likely to be decreased dry-season precipitation (Betts *et al.* 2008). The Andean flank of the Amazon

Thermokarst emerges across the permafrost tundra landscape.
Source: S. Kazlowski

is home to exceptional biodiversity, adjoins the most biodiverse regions of lowland Amazonia, and hosts a number of sheltered wet spots in otherwise dry areas. The cloud forests between 1,500 and 3,000 metres of elevation, considered to be a potentially disappearing climate, are susceptible to drying as cloud levels rise in the face of warming temperatures, and higher elevation restricted endemics would be particularly vulnerable (Killeen *et al.* 2007, Malhi *et al.* 2008).

Since Amazon forests appear vulnerable to increasing dryness, the potential for large carbon losses serving as positive feedbacks to climate change must be considered. According to some researchers, the exceptional growth in global atmospheric carbon dioxide (CO_2) concentrations in 2005, the third greatest in the global record, may have been partially caused by Amazon die-off resulting from drought effects effects (Cox *et al.* 2008, Phillips *et al.* 2009).

An annual increase of only 0.4 per cent in Amazon forest biomass roughly compensates for the entire fossil fuel emissions of Western Europe, so a switch from a moderate carbon sink to even a neutral state or a moderate carbon source would have significant implications on the build-up of CO_2 in the atmosphere. Considering that a 0.4 per cent of annual biomass sink represents the difference between two much larger values, the stand-level growth average approximating 2.0 per cent and mortality averaging of about 1.6 per cent, either a small decrease in growth or a small increase in mortality could shut the sink down (Phillips *et al.* 2008).

Peatlands and permafrost soils

The consequences of persistent climate warming of Arctic and subarctic terrestrial ecosystems, and associated processes, are ominous. The releases of carbon dioxide (CO_2), methane (CH_4), and more recently, nitrous oxide (N_2O) in these regions have accelerated in recent decades (Canadell and Raupach 2009).

Arctic permafrost soils store enormous amounts of carbon. Including all northern circumpolar regions, these ecosystems are estimated to hold twice as much carbon than is currently held in the atmosphere in the form of CO_2 (Zimov *et al.* 2006, UNEP 2008c, Schuur *et al.* 2008, Canadell and Raupach 2009). If Arctic warming accelerates as expected, one of the possible global implications of ensuing feedbacks is that ecosystems could cross critical thresholds as discussed in Earth Systems (Chapter One). Current warming in the Arctic is already causing increased emissions of CO_2 and CH_4 and feedbacks may have already begun (UNEP 2008c, UNEP 2009, Walter *et al.* 2007, Westbrook *et al.* 2009).

Most of the carbon released from thawing soils originates from the decomposition of organic matter—plant, animal, and microbial remains—deposited thousands of years ago. This organic matter has been kept relatively stable as a result of low temperatures in the permafrost in which it was trapped. As permafrost thaws, it creates thermokarst, a landscape of collapsed and subsiding ground with new or enlarged lakes, wetlands and craters on the surface (UNEP 2008c).

In this newly thawing landscape, upland areas with good drainage and oxygen available for microbial activity, are usually sources of CO_2. In the waterlogged areas and in lakes where anaerobic microbes decompose the organic matter, CH_4 becomes the dominant emission. Carbon emissions from Arctic terrestrial ecosystems are increasing because longer growing seasons and warmer temperatures support extended and vigorous plant growth. The interactions of these and other processes will determine the net effect of GHG emissions from the Arctic. Ultimately, Arctic emissions to the atmosphere will outpace potential carbon storage processes while changes in landscape will result in more of the Sun's energy being absorbed and released as heat, accelerating both global and local climate change (Canadell and Raupach 2009, Ise *et al.* 2008, Schuur *et al.* 2008, Canadell *et al.* 2007, Tarnocai *et al.* 2009).

Mountains

As climates change, sea levels rise, wetlands and drylands adjust, and ecosystems evolve, species seeking conditions that are cooler or that feature some other advantageous characteristics will move inland and upslope. Observations already demonstrate these trends (Parmesan 2006, Rosenzweig et al. 2008, Lenoir et al. 2008, Kelly and Goulden 2008). As these species adapt at higher altitudes, they may be classified as non-native—or even as invasive. The same characteristics that are advantages when recognizing resiliency and adaptability also identify weeds and invasive species.

Traditionally, biological invasions have been recognized as a major driver of biodiversity decline and altered ecosystem services in lowland regions where most studies have been conducted to document large-scale effects facilitated by human-mediated propagation (Dietz and Edwards 2006, Pauchard et al. 2009). In contrast, high-elevation environments seemed less affected by invasions—an assumption based on harsher climatic conditions and comparatively low human population densities. However, recent analysis estimates that over a thousand non-native species have become established in natural areas at high elevations worldwide, and although many of these are not considered invasive, some may threaten extant native mountain ecosystems (Pauchard et al. 2009).

In fact, recent studies have observed both rapid and significant shifts in plant distribution to high altitudes. The findings confirm a strong correlation between the observed changes in the distributional margins of these plant species with observed changes in regional climate conditions. Comparing surveys of plant cover from 1977 and 2007 along a 2,314 metre elevation gradient of California's Santa Rosa Mountains, researchers found that in just 30 years the average elevation of the dominant plant species expanded upward by 65 metres (Kelly and Goulden 2008). During that same period, southern California's climate experienced surface warming, increased precipitation variability, and a decrease in snow cover. The upward shifts were uniform across elevation, suggesting that the vegetation responded to a uniformly distributed causal factor. In addition, the vegetation shifts resulted in part from mortality during two distinguished periods of drought, implying a temporal sign-switching 'fingerprint' of climate change due to water balance. Following these lines of evidence, researchers attributed the shift to climate change rather than to either air pollution or fire (Kelly and Goulden 2008).

Another recent study across the temperate and Mediterranean mountain forests in western Europe revealed a similar upward shift in forest plant species. Here, researchers compared the altitudinal distribution of 171 plant species spanning from 0 to 2,600 metres above sea level. The results indicate a significant upward shift of 29 metres per decade in the optimum elevation of species over the 20th century (Lenoir et al. 2008).

As ecosystems shift, native species may adapt in ways that have the effect of an invasive species. Among insects especially, changing conditions may bring advantages that throw relationships evolved over millennia out of balance. Many insects in temperate zones are surviving at temperatures that inhibit their optimal metabolic capabilities. With warmer temperatures their reproductive seasons and rates may increase, with consequential increase in population. Many insect species also modulate metabolism to carbon dioxide availability and increasing atmospheric concentrations will grant advantage from that factor as well (DeLucia et al. 2008, Deutsch et al. 2008).

A 2008 study examined insect damage in over 5,000 fossil leaves from five different sites originating in the Paleocene-Eocene Thermal Maximum—an era of high carbon dioxide concentrations 55 million years ago. As carbon dioxide concentrations increased, so did the insect damage. When CO_2 concentrations decreased, the insect damage did as well. When CO_2 concentrations were at their peak, every leaf from

Figure 4.6: Total per cent coverage by perennial plants along the Deep Canyon Transect (Southern California's Santa Rosa Mountains) in 1977 and 2007

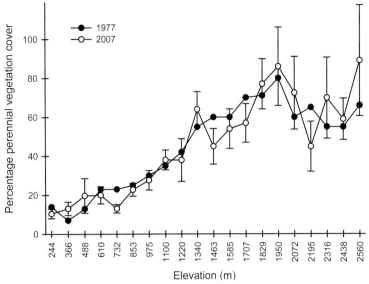

Source: Kelly and Goulden 2008

that time was severely damaged by herbivore insects. The researchers conclude that increased insect damage is likely to be a net long-term effect of anthropogenic atmospheric CO_2 increase and warming temperatures (Currano et al. 2008).

These findings have implications for human health as well as that of ecosystems. Increased duration of seasons and rates of reproduction in vectors of human disease are considered immediate threats to human health due to anthropogenic climate change (Huss and Fahrländer 2007, Costello et al. 2009, Clement et al. 2009).

ECOSYSTEM ADAPTATION

Ecosystems influence climate by affecting the energy, water, and carbon balance of the atmosphere at local and larger scales. However, current management efforts to mitigate climate change through ecosystem instruments focus on modification of one pathway, carbon sequestration. Using only one approach will only partially address the issue of ecosystem–climate interactions. The cooling of climate that results from carbon sequestration in forests may be partially negated by reduced surface albedo: This increases solar energy absorption, local longwave radiation, and local temperatures. Consideration of multiple interactions and feedbacks in climate management through ecosystems could lead to innovative climate-mitigation strategies, including GHG reductions primarily in industrialized nations, reduced desertification in arid zones, and reduced deforestation in the tropics. Each of these strategies has multiple ecological and societal benefits. Assessing their effectiveness requires better understanding of the interactions among feedback processes, their consequences at local and global scales, and the connections that link changes occurring at various scales in different regions (Chapin III et al. 2008).

Climate change threatens ecological systems at every scale throughout the world. Managing these systems in a way that ignores climate change will fail to meet the most basic management objectives. However, uncertainty in projected climate change impacts is one of the greatest challenges facing ecosystem managers. To select successful management strategies, managers need to understand the uncertainty inherent in projected climate impacts and how these uncertainties affect the outcomes of management activities. Perhaps the most important tool for managing ecological systems in the face of climate change is active adaptive management, in which systems are closely monitored and management strategies are altered to address expected and ongoing changes (Lawler et al. 2009).

SYSTEMS MANAGEMENT

Systems Management

A variety of actions are under discussion to manage the challenge posed by climate change: Cutting emissions, reforestation, and geoengineering are a few. Current research suggests that some of the possible actions are not only important but necessary for any chance of success—but no single action is sufficient on its own.

Chinese dyke-pond systems evolved over the past two thousand years, perfected by generations of farmers. Systems approach depends on maximizing internal inputs between land and water, optimizing efficient use of resources and minimizing waste. *Source: M. Harvey/Stillpictures*

As discussed in Earth Systems (Chapter One) at the beginning of this Compendium, scientists are becoming more and more concerned about the long-term trajectory of climate change effects. They realize that we are committed to centuries of climate impacts even with a solid management plan for cutting greenhouse gas emissions and returning concentrations to a reasonable level (Ramanathan and Feng 2008, Lenton *et al.* 2008, Smith *et al.* 2009, Solomon *et al.* 2009). Without an internationally accepted management strategy, how can we avoid counter-productive initiatives and maladaptations, ranging from legal impediments to wasted resources, possibly leading to famine, migration and conflict?

Combinations of management actions at scales ranging from local to global and from ecosystem adaptation to rebuilding infrastructure are needed to deal with climate change and its impacts. The necessary actions include a switch to environmentally sound energy sources; a halt to rampant deforestation in the tropics; sustainable management of fisheries, forests, agriculture, and other ecosystem services; and the development of innovative approaches to sequester carbon from the atmosphere over decades to millennia.

In 2007, the United Nations Foundation and Sigma Xi, the Scientific Research Society, prepared a report for the 15th session of the Commission on Sustainable Development with the intriguing title 'Confronting Climate Change: Avoiding the Unmanageable and Managing the Unavoidable' (SEG 2007). Adopting this conceptual approach to systems management for climate change is attracting attention from the policy-research community.

MANAGING THE UNAVOIDABLE

Through the use of innovative approaches in modelling and interdisciplinary analytical teams, scientists are beginning to design management systems that may enable the use of possible mitigation and adaptation actions at various scales in response to the changing climate.

Ecosystem adaptations

Current research suggests that business-as-usual will not work. For instance, until very recently, technology transfer to address climate change

has dwelled on mitigation issues. Given that the overwhelming majority of global greenhouse gas emissions are from the energy sector, energy alternatives became the dominant focus for technology transfer. Since energy technologies have been promoted as centralized and infrastructure dependent, it has been a priority on the part of developing country decision-makers to emulate developed country models by promoting infrastructure development, modernizing energy delivery, and stimulating private sector investment in large-scale installations. So technology transfer in the climate context has come to focus squarely on flows of experience, know-how, and equipment installation arrangements between countries, especially from developed to developing countries, and less on deployment and dissemination within countries and communities. Now that the question of technology for adaptation has moved into focus, some of the ideas about technology transfer for mitigation have been carried forward into the adaptation domain. However, this approach is not likely to work (Klein *et al.* 2006).

Adaptation requires responses at multiple scales. Building local resiliency in designated sectors and with acceptable socio-economic constraints on possible options offers many opportunities for stakeholder involvement and other community benefits. However, the rapid onset of climate change effects may forestall the gradual adaptation recommended (Klein *et al.* 2006).

While many decision-makers think of mitigation and adaptation as two independent paths in responding to climate change, recent work shows that adaptation and mitigation are closely linked. For example, on the one hand reforestation can be an effective net sink of carbon and therefore qualify as a mitigation measure. On the other hand, forests are also under threat from changing climate, and must therefore also adapt to climate change (Jackson *et al.* 2008).

Threats to forests can take many forms, including increases in temperature and growing seasons that encourage potentially threatening pests (Parkins and McKendrick 2007). In the northwestern region of North America, the

A recent photograph showing an example of pine tree disease and mortality: Pine trees turn red in the first year after mountain beetle infestation and grey in subsequent years. *Source: Kurz et al. 2008*

mountain pine beetle, *Dendroctonus ponderosae*, has been ravaging US and Canadian forest stands for nearly a decade. Their active populations have persisted because of warmer winters in which few beetle larvae are killed off by freezing temperatures. In addition, longer warm summers support more reproduction every year so larger populations of pine bark beetles are surviving to produce more offspring and to weaken the trees. Not only are the forests losing their ecosystem capacities to sustain water tables and avert soil erosion, but they are also turning from carbon sinks to carbon sources as more trees succumb to pests and begin to decompose (Kurz *et al.* 2008).

Box 5.1: Adaptation of natural systems

Our growing appreciation of ecosystem services and recognition of their economic as well as intrinsic value requires that we protect what we need and preserve as much as possible in the face of changing climate. In June of 2009, Resources for the Future published a broad review of challenges to terrestrial ecosystem adaptation to climate change. The authors presented a list of possible interventions that could be used to facilitate ecosystem adaptation with the intention to provoke discussion and stimulate innovative approaches. They focused on options realistic for the US where most semi-natural lands are managed by state and federal government agencies. Possible interventions could include:

Water management

The decline in the duration and extent of mountain seasonal snow will have progressively detrimental effects. One option for adaptation for stream systems may be to develop a large number of small high mountain water storage reservoirs in the upper cirques of the mountains just below the snowline. This activity was common before the advent of electrical grids and large dam complexes, when small dams, often only one to two metres high, were built to retain snowmelt for summer stream flow. A modern equivalent of small dams impounding areas of only a few hectares may be worth considering. Slow release of the impounded water from these dams would mimic the glacier and snow melt that has extended into the midsummer, providing stream flow all summer long. The ecological cost of this approach would be the loss of many high mountain meadows and timberline ecosystems, many of which would scarcely benefit from the increased water availability and could be damaged by construction activity.

Canadian Rocky Mountains in Banff National Park reflect in Herbert Lake near Lake Louise.
Photo Source: T. Dempsey/Photoseek.com

Vegetation management

Adaptations for natural forest and range management involve planting and cutting. In the US, the Department of Agriculture's Forest Service is planting more southern ecotypes of trees on the lands that are being manually replanted. Although there is some risk of getting "ahead" of the climate, much of the genetic variation in these trees revolves around cold hardiness dormancy timing and frost tolerance. Low daily temperatures are increasing faster than high temperatures. However, autumn temperatures are not increasing as fast as springtime temperatures. Therefore, this approach runs some risk for frost damage from early autumn freezes. Large-scale insect epidemics and large-scale wildfires are increasing dramatically in natural ecosystems. The primary proactive adaptation to these problems is more active forest thinning and vegetation harvesting. The approach is to have significantly less stressed forests of lower density, mimicking pre-fire suppression ecosystems.

Manage for resilience

More than a century of ecological research on ecosystem responses to biotic and abiotic conditions has clarified that the effects of climate change can only be understood in synergy with other human-caused stressors, including habitat fragmentation, roads, urbanization, and disease. Managing for resilience will require a focal species approach because species responses to climate change are and will be largely idiosyncratic. Some categories of focal species that might make the most appropriate targets for managed reduction of anthropogenic interference would include: (a) highly vulnerable species, (b) species with a high public profile, (c) data rich species, and (d) strongly interacting species.

Facilitate connectivity

Many species are unable to migrate due to habitat fragmentation or infrastructural barriers. Managing land to facilitate the movement of focal species beyond their current occupied range will preserve options for the species to adjust their geographic ranges and movement patterns under climate change. Large, contiguous, intact wildland regions provide large gradients of elevation and bioclimatic niches for species movement. However, even in human-dominated ecosystems, natural regions of parkland and riparian ecosystems may be critical for facilitating connectivity.

Directed evolution of native animals

Given the likelihood that those animals which will prosper in a changed climate are likely to be species humans consider to be invasive, pests, or overabundant, managers may need to consider a role for directed evolution. In essence, directed evolution would involve human mediated facilitation or acceleration of evolutionary adaptation to climate change. Livestock breeders, farmers, and gardeners always select their propagating stocks from individuals that manifest desired characteristics the cultivator wants to reproduce—directed evolution applies the same approach to undomesticated species.

Source: Running and Mills 2009

Box 5.2: Gene bank for a warming world

In February of 2008, the Norwegian Government officially opened an international seed depository near the town of Longyearbyen on Spitsbergen Island, in the Svalbard archipelago. The facility will provide secure long-term cold storage for preserving plant resources. Once completed, the Svalbard depository could maintain up to 4.5 million different seed varieties: ideally, samples of every variety of almost every important food crop in the world.

The vast collection is intended as insurance against disaster so food production can be restarted anywhere should it be threatened by a regional or global catastrophe. When the depository was originally conceived in the early 1980s, the perceived threats came from nuclear war and geopolitical uncertainty. When the idea resurfaced in 2002, following the adoption by the UN of the International Treaty on Plant Genetic Resources for Food and Agriculture, concerns about genetic resource loss from climate change brought new urgency and motivation to the concept.

The Svalbard facility will depend on seeds acquired according to strict protocols from sources around the world. If dried and packaged with the proper moisture content and stored at the right temperature, seeds from most major food crops will remain viable for hundreds to thousands of years. The seed collection will be maintained at optimal conditions for their long-term storage, maintained at a temperature of -18 degrees Celsius through the use of the naturally cold temperatures deep within Spitsbergen's permafrost and an artificial cooling system. The vault has been excavated out of sandstone—120 metres inside a mountain and lined with a metre of reinforced concrete. The facility is among the most energy-efficient and reliable structures in the world, with low operating costs and virtually no maintenance.

While no location can possibly provide 100 per cent insurance against the threat of natural and human dangers, Svalbard offers a level of protection that is difficult to match. At 78 degrees latitude—roughly 1,000 kilometres north of the northernmost tip of continental Norway—the location is suitably cold and isolated. The absence of volcanic or significant seismic activity in the region and the site's elevation above projected potential sea-level rise also contribute to the ideal longterm storage conditions.

The area also offers excellent infrastructure, including a dependable power supply and a nearby airport. Depositors retain ultimate ownership of the materials held in storage. However, the facility is owned by the Government of Norway and will be managed by the Nordic Gene Bank, which has been conserving seeds since 1984 in a facility located within an abandoned coal mine in Sweden.

Source: Fowler 2007, Skovmand 2007, UNEP 2008c

Figure 5.1: Decision framework for assessing possible species translocation

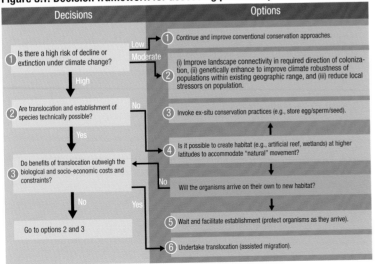

Assessing the feasibility of whether to attempt the movement of a species to prevent its extinction or ecosystem collapse. *Source: Hoegh-Guldberg et al. 2008*

Assisted colonization

Rapid climatic change has already forced changes to the distributions of many plants and animals, leading to severe range contractions and the potential extinction of some species (see Earth's Ecosystems, Chapter Four). The geographic ranges of many species are moving to higher latitudes and altitudes in response to shifts in the habitats to which these species have adapted over long periods. Some species already appear to be unable to disperse or adapt fast enough to keep up with the rates of climate change—currently happening at unprecedented rates for many living species. These organisms face increased extinction risk and whole ecosystems, such as cloud forests and coral reefs, may cease to function in their current form (Hoegh-Guldberg *et al.* 2007).

Previous discussions of conservation responses to climate change have considered assisted colonization as an option (McLachlan *et al.* 2007). Researchers have recently proposed the adoption of a risk assessment and management framework that could assist in identifying circumstances that require moderate action, such as enhancement of conventional conservation measures, or those that require more extreme action, such as assisted colonization.

One of the most serious risks associated with assisted colonization is the potential for creating new pest problems at the target site. Introduced organisms can also carry diseases and parasites or can alter the genetic structure and breeding systems of local populations (Hoegh-Guldberg *et al.* 2007, Running and Mills 2009).

In addition to the ecological risks, socio-economic concerns must be considered in decisions to move threatened species. Financial or human safety constraints, for example, may make a species' introduction undesirable. Current disputes already demonstrate that it is unacceptable to move threatened large carnivores into regions that are important for grazing livestock. Introduced plants that may affect the quantity or quality of grazing livestock output may also not be welcome. Using gene banks may be the only practical option for these and other species until more suitable habitat can be found or developed in the future. Currently, gene banks for agriculturally significant seeds have been established with consideration of conservation in a warming world. This approach needs to be applied to many more plants and animals that may not be of economic significance presently but that may prove invaluable in an uncertain future (Hoegh-Guldberg *et al.* 2007, Swaminathan 2009).

The reality of a rapidly changing climate has caught many natural-resource managers and policy-makers unprepared. Large-scale translocations might now be needed. Consequently, the conservation community needs to move beyond the preservation or restoration of species and ecosystems in place as the correct approach (Hoegh-Guldberg *et al.* 2007, Running and Mills 2009).

Assisted colonization will always carry some risk, but these must be weighed against those of extinction and ecosystem loss. Already some regions of the Earth such as the Arctic are experiencing high levels of warming. Many others will experience unprecedented heat within the next 100 years, as well as altered precipitation and ocean acidity. The future for some species and ecosystems is so uncertain that assisted colonization might be their best chance. These management decisions will require careful thought and will need to be backed up by detailed scientific understanding if they are to succeed (Hoegh-Guldberg *et al.* 2007, Running and Mills 2009).

Managed agricultural adaptation

Climate change threatens the sustainability of world agriculture. Its effects are likely to be unpredictable, making it particularly difficult for plant breeders, agronomists, and farmers to respond. As well as direct effects of changing climate on crops themselves, there will be indirect but potentially devastating pressures from weeds, pests, and diseases.

It is essential that everyone involved in sustaining food production be ready to meet this challenge. How mankind emerges from the coming century or more of predicted major shifts in climate will depend on how well agricultural production can be maintained (Sanghi and Mendelsohn 2008, Halford 2009).

Of the Earth's 130 million square kilometres of land, 12–15 million square kilometres are under crops, with another 35 million being grazed. Agriculture is a major economic, social, and cultural activity for billions of people, and it provides a wide range of ecosystem services. To meet projected growth in human population and per capita food demand, historical increases in agricultural production will have to continue, eventually doubling current production—a significant challenge even without the complexities introduced by the changing climate. Agriculture is highly sensitive to climate variations: Climate variability is the dominant source of production unreliabilities from year to year in many regions, and persists as a source of disruption to ecosystem services (Howden *et al.* 2007).

However, that climate variability has led to the development of an immense diversity of agricultural practices along with cultural, institutional, and economic factors. This means there is a correspondingly large array of possible adaptation options to meet the challenges of climate change.

Over the next four decades, the amount of available cropland per person is projected to drop to less than 1,000 square metres, due to biological limits, requiring an increase in agricultural production that is unattainable through conventional means (Montgomery 2008). A sense of urgency has been growing, in response to the universal decline of soil quality that results from various systems of intensive agriculture. The problem of soil degradation, which has affected 84 per cent of the world's croplands, presents serious implications for agricultural productivity and broader ecosystem services (Hazell and Wood 2008).

An emerging body of scientific research focuses on spatially integrated management approaches to agriculture. This would involve a move away from the conventional model of land-use segregation, in which some areas are dedicated wholesale to food production, while others are set aside for conservation or other uses (Scherr and McNeely 2008, Holden *et al.* 2008). For decades, biodiversity conservation and agricultural productivity were thought to be incompatible and mutually exclusive pursuits. But practitioners of eco-agriculture challenge these notions. Their approach transforms large-scale, high-input monoculture plantations at the farm level to a more diverse, low-input, and integrated system at the landscape level. Given the necessary management, policy, and governance structures, these new eco-agricultural land-use mosaics could support biodiversity while meeting increasing demands for wider ecosystem services and achieving critical goals of agricultural sustainability (Scherr and McNeely 2008). By treating food production as just one of many possible ecosystem services, eco-agriculture in a sense encourages landholders to cultivate clean air and water, rich soil, and biological diversity, as well as food. The local and regional resilience this produces is also the basis of well-managed adaptation to climate change.

Forms of eco-agriculture have been practised in the past and at impressive scales: Terra Preta soils of central Amazonia could provide tremendous opportunities for multiple benefits (UNEP 2009). Large-scale generation and utilization of nutrient-rich Terra Preta soils would decrease the necessity for clearing new agricultural lands that require deforestation. Less deforestation for agricultural lands would maintain biodiversity while mitigating both land degradation and climate change and, if done properly, can alleviate waste and sanitation problems in some communities (Glaser 2007).

Multiple challenges for agriculture

In spring 2008, precipitous increases in staple food prices, which threatened the lives of tens of millions, provoked demonstrations and food riots in 37 countries and were attributed by some to projections for biofuel demand created by a response to climate change. These events may signal the arrival of an era in which longstanding relative inequalities have reached a breaking point for the global poor. It has become clear that ecosystem management and food security are intimately linked. The surplus living resources and ecological margin of error in many regions are gone. As societies struggle over diminishing tracts of fertile and irrigable land—and over traditional fishing grounds—the accelerating threats of changing climate, ecosystem collapse, and population stress have converged in a way that calls the very future of food availability into question. The debates are vigorous and highly contentious. The issue of food security created global political panic in 2008 and will no doubt continue to occupy much of the international agenda for years to come (UNEP 2009).

There is no denying the achievements of past agricultural intensification in the mid to late 20th century. The economic and social advances that characterize India, China, and much of Latin America today are, to a significant degree, due to that agricultural intensification. The problem is that while the global agricultural system that emerged is undeniably more productive, in a mid 20th century sense, its practice has accelerated soil erosion, soil salination, nitrification of water bodies, and overuse of synthetic pesticides with subsequent loss of natural pest control and other ecosystem services affecting agricultural sustainability. At the same time,

Woman prepares for planting at the Mshikamano women's group-farm in Bagamoyo, Tanzania, where eco-agricultural practices are used to promote both conservation and rural development strategies. *Source: T. Thompson*

these intense agricultural practices have contributed to the burden of GHG concentrations in the atmosphere—producing the changing climate now threatening those socio-economic achievements.

Our agricultural systems' distribution flaws—based on fossil-fuelled cheap transportation—make whole populations vulnerable to supply shocks as witnessed in 2008 (Surowiecki 2008). Despite higher crop yields in many countries, there are vast, persistent, and widening gaps in the ability of societies to feed themselves, much less to protect future resources and ecosystem services (Hazell and Wood 2008). For most developing countries, entrenched and deepening poverty stems from the fact that millions of small-scale farmers, many of whom are women, are simply unable to grow enough food to sustain their families, their communities, or their countries (AGRA 2008, Ngongi 2008). The efficiencies derived from the economy of scale in intensified agricultural systems do not apply at the scale of these families and communities (Dossani 2008).

As the human population continues to grow, the pool of land available for agricultural production shrinks, and climate change disrupts expected precipitation patterns, the costs and efforts required to avert a worst-case global food crisis will inevitably increase for developing countries. A number of institutions and research bodies are pressing for a complete rethink of the role of agriculture in achieving equitable development and sustainability. Increasingly, they are advocating approaches to agriculture that recognize the importance of multiple ecosystem services and that build resilience in the face of the changing climate.

The extensive 2008 International Assessment of Agricultural Knowledge, Science and Technology for Developement (IAASTD) report advocates a radical move away from technologically-based production enhancements to a focus on the needs of small farmers in diverse ecosystems, particularly in areas of high vulnerability to climate change and other threats to ecosystems. Recognizing that the poor have benefited the least from increased productivity, the study argues for improving rural livelihoods, empowering marginalized stakeholders, enhancing ecosystem services,

integrating diverse knowledge, providing more equitable market access for the poor, and building climate resilience (IAASTD 2008). In November 2008, the UN's Food and Agricultural Organization (FAO) called for an immediate plan of action on a new 'World Agricultural Order' to ensure that production meets rising demand in the face of climate change, while safeguarding the goals of sustainable ecosystem management (FAO 2008). It proposed a new governance system for world food security and agricultural trade that offers farmers, in developed and developing countries alike, the means of earning a decent living (Diouf 2008).

While increased chemical and technological inputs may keep the agricultural production system going over the short-term, it becomes progressively more difficult to sustain (Montgomery 2008, Pretty 2008). In the context of climate change and how it is affecting Earth's Systems now as demonstrated by physical and ecosystem shifts, the evolving reality will compel those responsible for the new agricultural paradigm to reach a balance between production and ecosystem integrity. If we can establish the balance sooner, we will avoid the inevitable shocks and panics that result from business-as-usual practices—and we will avoid famine, migration, and conflict that could result from agricultural incapacity (Montgomery 2008).

Management of terrestrial biomass

Maintaining ecosystem integrity is gaining new importance as a basis for sustainable agriculture. At the same time, agricultural principles can be applied to forestry and soil ecosystem services, when they are regarded as potential carbon sinks that can be enhanced through conscientious management practices. Such sustainable management practices aim for long-term sequestration capacities while maintaining ecosystem service cycles on the shorter term for supporting local communities and their interactions in a globalized economy. As noted by some researchers, sustainable forest management practices can maximize carbon sequestration rates and then provide harvests as carbon accumulation dwindles for exploitation as

Tropical rainforest at Tambopata Nature Reserve, Peru.
Source: S. Muller/ Still Pictures

low GHG fuel through advanced combustion or as long-term construction products that replace high carbon intensity concrete and steel materials (Fahey *et al.* 2009, Liu and Han 2009). Innovative soil sequestration approaches can keep carbon out of the atmosphere for millennia while locally mitigating soil degradation problems that affect 84 per cent of the world's arable land (Montgomery 2008, UNEP 2009, Bruun *et al.* 2009).

Carbon sequestration in forests

Carbon is stored in forest ecosystems in the form of living tree biomass and dead organic matter. In most forests, the largest carbon pools are above-ground live biomass and mineral soil organic matter, with smaller amounts in roots and surface detritus.

Currently, forests are major contributors to the terrestrial ecosystems that remove about 3 billion tonnes of anthropogenic carbon from the atmosphere every year through net growth, absorbing about 30 per cent of all CO_2 emissions from fossil fuel burning and net deforestation (IPCC 2007c, Karsenty *et al.* 2008, Ceccon and Miramontes 2008). The 40 million square kilometres of forest ecosystems, almost a third of the Earth's total land area, store reservoirs of carbon holding more than twice the amount of carbon in the atmosphere.

Scientists and policy makers agree there are a number of major strategies available to mitigate carbon emissions through forestry management activities (Canadell and Raupach 2008). First, reforestation and afforestation increase total forested land area. China has cultivated 240,000 square kilometres of new and regrown forest during the 20th century, transforming net carbon emissions to net gains of nearly 180 million tonnes of carbon per year and offsetting 21 per cent of Chinese fossil fuel emissions in 2000 (Wang *et al.* 2007, Gregg *et al.* 2008).

Second, increasing the carbon density of existing forests at both stand and landscape scales enhances the effectiveness of forested area. Fire suppression and harvest exclusion in US forests during the 20th century led to a 15 per cent increase in forest biomass between 1927 and 1990, although the policy was not implemented for the purpose of carbon sequestration (Canadell and Raupach 2008).

Third, optimizing the use of forest products to substitute for other fossil-fuel CO_2 emissions: At a larger scale, this may mean using lumber instead of concrete for some building purposes. But it can also affect fire reduction policies that require the removal of undergrowth and occasional thinning by local communities to contribute to fuel needs among those who harvest the 'windfall' (UNEP 2008c).

Finally, reducing deforestation has high potential for cost-effective contributions to climate protection. The continued destruction of Earth's tropical forests alone accounts for an estimated 17 per cent of all GHG emissions. Under the reducing emissions from deforestation and forest degradation (REDD) scheme, developing countries with tropical forests would participate in a new international carbon market to receive compensation for reducing and stabilizing national deforestation rates (Canadell and Raupach 2008, UNEP 2009).

Significant uncertainty defines the future size and stability of the terrestrial carbon stock in the context of climate change and possible feedbacks (Bonan 2008, Jackson *et al.* 2008, Rhemtulla *et al.* 2009). Most global climate-carbon coupled models for the 21st century indicate some carbon accumulation in biomass, largely from a CO_2 fertilization effect on certain types of plants. However, there are uncertainties about the outcome from interacting variables (Canadell *et al.* 2007, Canadell and Raupach 2008). Regions with large carbon stores that are vulnerable to climate change have been identified that could lead to the release of billions of tonnes of carbon by the end of this century: Not only the possible releases from northern landscapes and continental shelves, but also from peat swamp forests in Southeast Asia where climate models agree on a future drying trend (Li *et al.* 2007).

Forest management practices affect net carbon exchange with the atmosphere, both by changing the amount of carbon stored in various pools and by altering the trajectory of net ecosystem productivity at a location. Sustainable forest management can increase total carbon sequestration because much of the carbon in wood products removed during forest harvest is not returned immediately to the atmosphere, but is stored in durable products and more trees can be grown to sequester more carbon (Liu and Han 2009). Theoretically, maintaining the landscape in the optimal stages of net ecosystem productivity can maximize carbon sequestration. This is accomplished by managing for maximum tree stocking and by using the harvested wood for durable products or as a substitute for fossil fuels. The overall effect of forest management on GHG emissions depends on the type of forest, the type of wood products, and the efficiency of biomass conversion. Assumptions about how the wood and wood residues will substitute for other products that embody greater carbon intensity in their manufacture or their consumption as fuel must also be considered (Eriksson *et al.* 2007, Fahey *et al.* 2009).

Box 5.4: Reducing emissions from deforestation and forest degradation

Since the close of the IPCC's Fourth Assessment Report, a growing amount of worldwide research has been devoted to the mitigative and adaptive capacities of forests. Experts suggest that the active protection of tropical forests is not only a crucial ecosystem management priority, but also a cost-effective means of reducing overall emissions (UNEP 2009). This has given rise to the concept of "reducing emissions from deforestation and forest degradation" (REDD). For instance, reducing rates of deforestation by 50 per cent by 2050, and stopping deforestation when countries reach 50 per cent of their current forested area, would avoid emissions equivalent to 50 billion tonnes of carbon (Gullison *et al.* 2007, UNEP 2009). As pressures build for a global policy for mitigating GHG emissions, an international mechanism for REDD implementation is likely to emerge as a central component of an optimal climate change treaty (Oestreicher *et al.* 2009, UNEP 2009).

However, including REDD in a new climate treaty raises many difficult institutional, methodological, and scientific issues (Strassburg *et al.* 2009, Preskett *et al.* 2008). For example, robust, reliable and regular estimation of forest emissions from deforestation and degradation is a crucial requirement of REDD policy, which has not yet been realized (Howes 2009). To verify the uptake of carbon by a particular forest, it will be necessary to develop new tools that are both inexpensive and accurate, but not easily dissembled or manipulated. Another difficult issue concerns the question of governance of forests and the need to find equitable models of land tenure and land use rights under a REDD policy (IUFRO 2009, UNEP 2009).

There are other aspects of REDD policy that will be less difficult to implement. For example, it will be fairly easy from a technical standpoint to verify the quantity of wood used from a particular forest as a substitute for carbon-intensive building materials or fossil fuels. However, some technical issues remain, for instance, regarding the permanence of the forest, and about spinoff effects of using wood as a substitute material (Fahey *et al.* 2009).

Many questions remain about national capacities and institutional preparedness to carry out REDD policies. It is wrong to assume, for example, that all developing countries are willing or able to implement REDD policies (Schrope 2009).

Finally, in the rush to introduce REDD policies, it is important not to sidetrack the beneficial trend towards sustainable forest management which calls for multiple benefits from using forests including social, intrinsic, and non-market values. Sustainable forest management also puts high value on the ecosystem services provided by forests and on incorporating indigenous knowledge into forest management. REDD policies should reinforce rather than undermine sustainable forest management practices. (Howes 2009).

Figure 5.2: Carbon storage in terrestrial ecosystems

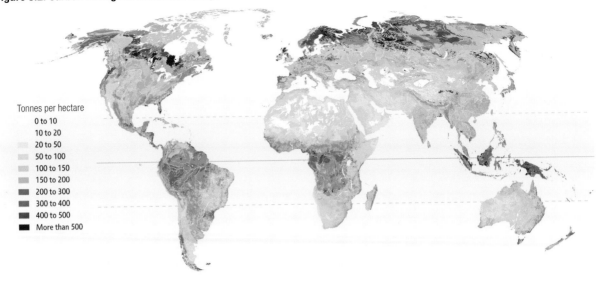

Tonnes per hectare
- 0 to 10
- 10 to 20
- 20 to 50
- 50 to 100
- 100 to 150
- 150 to 200
- 200 to 300
- 300 to 400
- 400 to 500
- More than 500

Terrestrial ecosystems store about 2,100 Gigatonnes of carbon in living organisms, litter, and soil organic matter. This is more than twice the amount currently present in the atmosphere. *Source: Trumper et al. 2009, Ruesch and Gibbs 2008*

Long-term sequestration in soils

An innovative approach to soil carbon sequestration has emerged that may offer a low-risk and very efficient way to mitigate climate change and replenish soil fertility. The concept involves producing biologically derived charcoal, or biochar, and incorporating it into soils. Biochar is essentially the product of cooking biomass at low temperature and in the absence of oxygen, so it turns into charcoal.

Early research suggests that biochar sequestration may not only keep CO_2 from reaching the atmosphere, but could also extract CO_2 from the atmosphere (McHenry 2009, Gaunt and Lehmann 2008, Bruun *et al.* 2009). In addition, the prolonged decomposition of biochar—centuries to millennia—enhances soil fertility and other properties of soil quality including increased water retention and cation exchange capacities (Bruun *et al.* 2009).

The idea for using biochar as a response to today's climate change challenge originates from traditional ecological knowledge. Pre-Columbian inhabitants of the central Amazon basin made Terra Preta—Portuguese for dark earth. These dark, nutrient-rich soils were manufactured by mixing large amounts of charred residue, organic wastes, manure, and bone into relatively infertile soil. By controlling low-temperature, low-oxygen smoldering fires at the surface of the soils, the prehistoric soil managers were able to carbonize the majority of the accumulated biomass and produce a rich Terra Preta.

Terra Preta soils are three times more concentrated in their organic matter, nitrogen, and phosphorous content, and 70 times more rich in mineralized carbon than the surrounding nutrient-depleted soils. The half-life of the charcoal in Terra Preta soils is estimated at thousands of years (Kleiner 2009, UNEP 2009). Today, research scientists are refining the techniques of this early tradition with the aim of developing biochar production technologies as a tool that could lock carbon for similar millennial time-periods.

To better understand the optimal benefits of biochar sequestration, it is important to distinguish between how CO_2 is released and captured through the lifecycle of plant growth, a process that is considered carbon

Box 5.5: Advanced wood combustion at the community scale

The use of wood fuel in advanced combustion facilities is supplying a significant proportion of heat and electricity needs from locally grown and renewable resources—a long sought-after goal. Advanced wood combustion has been contributing to energy needs in Scandinavia for decades and the system is now expanding in France, Germany, and other European countries. Community-scale wood energy combustion can add financial value to local forest stands, support restoration and improvement in the form of selective harvesting, and provide local employment. Sustainability of local forests needs careful monitoring to assure that forest-energy outputs enhance rather than deplete ecosystems. Ideally, combustion and pollution are controlled by technical advances in wood-energy development. In the 2000s, Austria's 1,000 advanced wood combustion facilities emit minimal pollutant emissions because of the high-quality combustion control and wood's low pollutant content compared to fossil fuels.

Source: Hackstock 2008, Richter et al. 2009

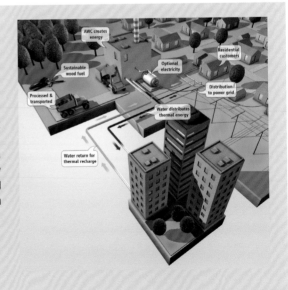

'neutral', and the biochar approach which has a 'negative' net effect. Through the process of photosynthesis, Earth's terrestrial plants absorb approximately 60.6 billion tonnes of carbon every year. A similar amount of carbon is then released back into the atmosphere through respiration. Biochar sequestration, by comparison, is carbon negative, as it results in a long-term withdrawal of CO_2 from the atmosphere by diverting a portion of the carbon out of the photosynthesis cycle and into a much slower, stable, and resistant state of mineralized carbon.

Recent studies have improved our understanding of the biochar mechanisms for mineralizing carbon. However, most scientists concede that the rates of subsequent demineralization through chemical breakdown are not thoroughly understood (Gaunt and Lehmann 2008, Bruun *et al.* 2009). However, farmers are moving ahead with the use of biochar because of its ability to reinvigorate degraded soils. A biochar product with the brand name 'Agrichar' has been marketed as a product from a patented pyrolysis process.

According to a study which examined the viability of 17 carbon management and geoengineering options, biochar has the potential to sequester nearly 400 billion tonnes of carbon over the 21st century, reducing atmospheric CO_2 concentrations by 37 parts per million (Lenton and Vaughan 2009). Although some researchers caution that these numbers are likely high, even the most conservative estimates of 20 billion tonnes of carbon sequestered by 2030 could have a significant impact on atmospheric GHG concentrations. Biochar could be an essential component of systems management necessary for meeting the climate change challenge (Kleiner 2009, Lehmann 2007).

AVOIDING THE UNMANAGEABLE

Society has very important decisions to make. Even if GHG emissions ceased immediately, the warming of the Earth and associated changes—as well as those of ocean acidifcation—would continue beyond this century and perhaps this millennium (SEG 2007, Ramanathan and Feng 2008, Smith *et al.* 2009, Solomon *et al.* 2009). Management practice decisions for addressing such monumental issues must be effective, efficient, and equitable, within the realization that there are no instantaneous solutions.

We know the necessary components of any comprehensive management strategy: A switch to environmentally sound energy sources; a halt to rampant deforestation in the tropics; sustainable management of fisheries, forests, agriculture, and other ecosystem services; and development of innovative approaches to carbon sequestration from the atmosphere over decades to millennia. These are necessary components but may not be sufficient to prevent dangerous anthropogenic climate change. Additional, not alternative, schemes are under discussion that need very serious and considered decisions to be made—by society.

Geoengineering

Large-scale physical interventions, or technological fixes on a planetary scale, are proposed actions addressing climate change grouped under the term geoengineering. Proposals to manipulate the global climate intend to correct the Earth's radiative imbalance either through capturing and sequestering carbon out of the atmosphere or through reducing the amount of incoming shortwave solar radiation (Lenton and Vaughan 2009, Victor *et al.* 2009).

Carbon dioxide removal (CDR) techniques are designed to extract CO_2 from the atmosphere while solar radiation management (SRM) techniques reflect a small percentage of the Sun's light back into space to offset the effects of increased GHG concentrations (Royal Society 2009). CDR concepts are based on the carbon sequestration accomplished by nature through photosynthesizing plants and other organisms. SRM concepts are based on the natural effects observed in the atmosphere after powerful volcanic eruptions.

Figure 5.3: Biochar can be carbon negative

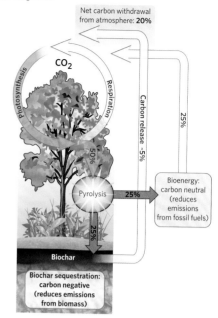

One method for the removal of CO_2 from the atmosphere is 'iron fertilization'. This exploits the CO_2 sequestration potential in parts of the ocean that are nutrient rich but do not support plankton growth due to a lack of iron. Supplying large amounts of iron to these areas of the ocean could stimulate plankton blooms that theoretically will bind carbon molecules and eventually sequester them on the deep sea-floor. Many small-scale experiments have been conducted over the last two decades that show some success at producing plankton blooms. These experiments have invoked strong reactions, both for and against the concept. The most serious concern, voiced by scientists, is the possible disruption in nutrient cycles that feed ocean life. This would constitute a serious challenge to marine ecosystems already overexploited and endangered by human activities. In November 2007, the Convention on the Prevention of Marine Pollution stated that "...planned operations for large-scale fertilization operations using micronutrients—for example, iron—to sequester carbon dioxide are currently not justified" (IMO 2007, UNEP 2008c).

Another potential ocean-based approach to CO_2 removal is the manipulation of the overturning circulation of the oceans to increase the rate of sequestration of atmospheric carbon into the deep sea. Vertical pipes would pump nutrient-rich deep water to the surface, enhancing upwelling rates and promoting the downwelling of dense water in the subpolar oceans (Lovelock and Rapley 2007). A potential drawback is that the manner in which altering natural circulation patterns locally will affect the overall carbon balance is unknown and could lead to release, rather than sequestration, through upwelling of carbon from the deep ocean (Royal Society 2009, Yool *et al.* 2009).

A land-based approach involves completely artificial CO_2 collectors that emulate the sequestration capability of photosynthesizing plants. Based on a technology used in fish tank filters and developed by scientists from Columbia University's Earth Institute, a method called 'air capture' would remove CO_2 directly from the atmosphere at the location of the ideal geological deposits for storage. In a project in Iceland, CO_2 is collected from a local industrial process and injected into the underlying basalt formations, rich in magnesium and calcium, with the goal of reproducing the natural processes that form calcite and dolomite deposits and binding carbon molecules for millions of years. These formation types are common on every continent (Gislason *et al.* 2007). Whether this scheme

Ordinary biomass fuels are carbon neutral–the carbon captured in the biomass by photosynthesis returns to the atmosphere within decades through natural processes such as decomposition or by burning as fuel. Biochar systems can be carbon negative because they retain a substantial portion of carbon fixed by plants and mineralize it so its chemical breakdown spans millennia.
Source: Lehmann 2007

Figure 5.4: Geoengineering options

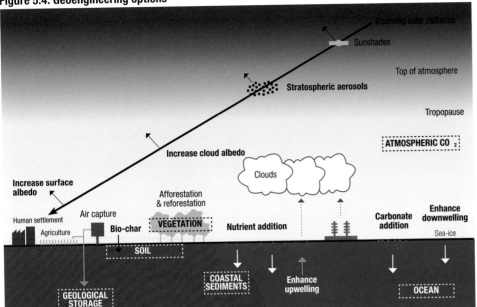

Schematic overview of the climate geoengineering proposals considered. Black arrowheads indicate shortwave radiation, white arrowheads indicate enhancement of natural flows of carbon, grey downward arrow indicates engineered flow of carbon, grey upward arrow indicates engineered flow of water, dotted vertical arrows illustrate source of cloud condensed nuclei, and dashed boxes indicate carbon storage. *Source: adapted from Lenton and Vaughan 2009*

becomes a viable contribution to solving the climate crisis will depend on the success of the ongoing experiments, as well as the regulatory constraints involved (IMO 2007, Morton 2007, Lackner and Liu 2008).

Aerosol injection schemes are designed to artificially increase aerosol levels in the stratosphere, causing an overall increase in planetary reflectivity. The method using sulphate aerosols simulates the effect of large volcanic eruptions on global climate in reducing incoming solar radiation and has been the subject of climate geoengineering proposals for some time (Robock 2008b, Royal Society 2009, Hegerl and Solomon 2009).

Suggested methods for delivering the required amount of sulphate aerosols to the stratosphere include aircraft, aircraft/rocket combinations, artillery and balloons and could carry an annual cost of tens of billions of dollars (Blackstock *et al.*

2009). The environmental impacts of the delivery system itself would also need to be factored into the feasibility analyses of such schemes (Robock 2008a, Royal Society 2009).

The increase in reflectivity of the stratospheric layer after the eruption of Mount Pinatubo in 1991 was also shown to affect the hydrological cycle, producing droughts through a drop in global precipitation levels during 1992 (Trenberth and Dai 2007). Detailed ocean-atmosphere modelling has indicated that enhancing stratospheric sulphate aerosols would reduce the precipitation of the Asian and African summer monsoons, potentially affecting more than a billion people (Robock 2008a, Rasch *et al.* 2008, Tilmes *et al.* 2008).

An enhanced layer of sulphate aerosols also reduces stratospheric ozone levels, with global ozone levels about 2 per cent below expected values after the eruption of Mount Pinatubo (Robock 2008a). Geoengineering through stratospheric sulphate aerosols could lead to a substantial increase in Arctic ozone depletion, possibly delaying the recovery of the layer by up to 70 years (Tilmes *et al.* 2008).

Sunshade geoengineering is the proposed installation of space-based sunshields or reflective mirrors to deflect a proportion of incoming solar radiation before it reaches the atmosphere. Sunlight deflectors would either be placed in near-Earth orbits or near the Lagrange point, about 1.5 million kilometres from Earth where the gravitational pull of the Earth and Sun are equal. An array of sunshades in this position would pose less of a threat to Earth-orbiting satellites than near-Earth objects. Recent modelling has demonstrated that sunshade engineering could be successful (Lunt *et al.* 2008).

Schemes to increase reflectivity at the Earth's surface by covering deserts with reflective films, painting roofs white, or generating low-level cloud cover over oceans either all have risky side effects or only local effects (Royal Society 2009, Hegerl and Solomon 2009).

Box 5.6: Carbon Capture and Storage

Carbon Capture and Storage (CCS) is a method for the geological sequestration of carbon dioxide (CO_2). CCS systems are designed to capture CO_2 emissions where they are most concentrated at industrial point sources such as coal power generation plants and to transport it to storage reservoirs.

In theory, the captured CO_2 would be compressed into a liquid, then pumped through a pipeline or transported on a ship to a site where it would be injected into the target reservoir. The injection technology already exists and is used in an oil field optimization technique: When an oil or gasfield has become depleted and the remaining fossil hydrocarbon lacks pressure to reach the wellhead, CO_2 is injected into the far side of the reservoir to put pressure on the remaining fossil hydrocarbon, pushing it towards the wellhead where it is brought to the surface. This technique is called enhanced oil recovery and has been used by the oil and gas industry for decades. These depleted oil and gas reservoirs have been suggested as suitable CO_2 destinations, as have deep saline formations and unexploitable coal seams (Lenton and Vaughan 2009).

Other storage methods under investigation include the direct injection of CO_2 into the deep oceans where it is assumed the high pressure will keep any CO_2 from leaking to the surface—or into the ocean itself and contributing to ocean acidification and resulting marine ecosytem crises. Another suggested destination involves mineral carbonation, which would combine minerals with concentrated CO_2 to form carbonate crystals. All these methods are still regarded as experimental in terms of storing large amounts of CO_2, and their effectiveness is unknown. Also their possible environmental impacts are not yet known (Blackford *et al.* 2009).

CCS will require significant expenditures on equipment and infrastructure to capture, transport, and store the compressed CO_2. Large pipeline networks are expensive but even without such considerations the main problems involve the size, location, accessibility, and reliability of suitable geological reservoirs. The risks of subsequent carbon leakage and the potential for interactions with groundwater are another unknown and could be prohibitive.

Recent modelling results from the International Energy Agency suggest that CCS could provide 20 per cent of total GHG emission reductions in 2050 under advantageous economic conditions (IEA 2008a, IEA 2008b). However, a 2009 analysis of CCS start-up costs determine the price of avoided CO_2 would be US\$ 120 to 180 per tonne (Al-Juaied and Whitmore 2009).

Although implementing any of the SRM proposals could take decades, the cooling effect they are designed to achieve would be relatively rapid, with atmospheric temperatures responding within a few years once the apparatus was in place (Matthews and Caldeira 2007). The SRM methods may therefore provide a useful tool for reducing global temperatures rapidly should catastrophic climate changes begin. However, such systems would require a huge commitment of resources given the need for constant upkeep over the period of their implementation, since any failure or 'switching off' of an SRM scheme could result in rapid warming (Robock 2008a).

Without a reduction of GHG concentrations in the atmosphere, other direct effects of increased CO_2—particularly ocean acidification and the collapse of marine ecosystems —remain unmitigated. The logistical and technical considerations of space-based geoengineering, plus the uncertainties in costs, effectiveness, risks and timescales of implementation make these measures unfeasible as solutions to dangerous climate change in the short-term (Royal Society 2009).

Another consideration that geoengineering approaches must address is liability: Who or what company, agency, government, or institution is responsible for unfortunate side effects that may result from deliberate interference with Earth Systems? The legal issues behind geoengineering are likely to pose more of a problem than the technical challenges of implementing such an endeavour (Royal Society 2009).

Carbon dioxide removal methods may be preferable to solar radiation management methods because they involve fewer risks and uncertainties. Although CDR methods have the advantage of returning the climate system closer to its natural state, none of the methods has yet proved effective at an affordable cost and with acceptable side effects (Royal Society 2009).

Given these wide ranging implications that must be kept under consideration of geoengineering schemes—as well as the potential to overshoot the effects on Earth Systems by underestimating climate sensitivity—experimentation must be strictly controlled and liabilities must be delineated. Deploying a well-planned and closely controlled solar radiation management scheme could be an option for a worst case climate scenario. However, some kind of carbon dioxide removal methods must be explored as well, including aggressive afforestation programmes, use of soil amendments such as biochar, and construction of carbon extraction towers over geological sinks. Considering how difficult it has been to reach agreement on the obvious climate challenge solutions based on common but differentiated responsibilities, the uncertainties involved in geoengineering schemes may prohibit any global agreement on deliberately interfering with Earth's Systems (Boyd 2008, Royal Society 2009, Jackson 2009).

Among the research findings and the analysis that scientists have been discussing over the past few years, a significant proportion is now addressing issues of irreversibility and commitment to climate effects that will last for centuries if not a millennium. Abrupt change, tipping elements, and cumulative effects concern the analysis more and more. In this Compendium, we see evidence of thousands of marine and terrestrial species already stressed by climate change effects. Discussion has opened on decision frameworks for assisted colonization, gene banks for storing material from species which cannot be relocated, and launching what would normally be considered pollutants into the atmosphere. These trends communicate a sense of alarm among the scientists and practitioners who are most familiar with the science of climate change.

CONTINUING SCIENTIFIC ROLE

The necessary management practices to respond to climate change include a switch to environmentally sound energy sources; a halt to rampant deforestation in the tropics; sustainable management of fisheries, forests, agriculture, and other ecosystem services; and the development of innovative approaches to sequester carbon from the atmosphere over decades to millennia. While none of these options is sufficient to address the challenge, each must be part of the strategy. Another necessary component in any effective response to climate change must be to continue supporting, and even expanding, the admirable efforts that our scientists have been exerting in attempts to comprehend Earth System Science.

In 2008, authors of the IPCC Fourth Assessment Report (AR4) met with representatives from the Global Climate Observing System (GCOS), the World Climate Research Programme (WCRP), and the International Geosphere-Biosphere Programme (IGBP) to discuss needs for future climate change research and observations in the context of what was learned from the IPCC AR4 process. Participants agreed to 11 key priorities for science and climate change that, if fulfilled, would advance us well on our way to further understanding of how climate is changing and how we can respond. As scientists continue to ask themselves how to fill gaps and to better examine the complexities of natural systems, they will continue to lead us in what has been termed the greatest challenge of the 21st century: Addressing climate change.

Box 5.7: Key priorities for science of climate change

1. Improve process-level understanding, climate models, observations of climate-relevant parameters and climate monitoring systems in specific areas.

2. Make climate information more relevant to decisions concerning impacts, adaptation and mitigation.

3. In addition to global, decadal predictions, increase focus on regional-scale climate information, accounting for land surface processes and biosphere–atmosphere interactions.

4. Climate and impact relevant observational data records should be reprocessed to reflect new knowledge and to improve the flagging of errors and estimation of biases; and incorporated into reanalysis efforts.

5. Datasets must be expanded to include observations of the impacts of climate change and to account for autonomous or planned adaptation, especially highly vulnerable regions.

6. A systematic approach must be established specifically to monitor and assess vulnerability.

7. Develop and apply a consistent, harmonized set of scenarios of land use, land cover, and emissions databases to support both the climate and integrated assessment communities, with consistency across spatial and temporal scales, and considering both historic and future timescales.

8. Observations and innovative technology should be utilized to better understand variations in the hydrologic cycle, both in the very short-term and sustained over decades, particularly with respect to extremes.

9. Establish a community initiative that uses physical process studies, observations, and syntheses to obtain a consensus on the possible nonlinear responses of ice sheets to climate change, including their influences on rates of sea-level rise.

10. Improve process modelling and understanding of feedbacks in the carbon cycle across the Earth Systems.

11. Improve understanding of the processes involved in aerosol indirect forcing (e.g., aerosol transport, convective processes, cloud formation and dissipation) to represent them reliably in climate models.

Source: Doherty et al. 2009

Glossary

Acidification
Change in the environment's natural chemical balance caused by an increase in the concentration of acidic elements. The main source of acidifying substances which include sulphur dioxide (SO_2), nitrogen oxides (NO_x), and ammonia (NH_3) is emissions from fossil fuel combustion.

Adaptation
Adjustment in natural or human systems over time to a new or changing environment, including anticipatory and reactive adaptation, private and public adaptation, and autonomous and planned adaptation.

Albedo
Fraction of solar radiation reflected by a surface or object, often expressed as a percentage. Snow-covered surfaces have a high albedo, the surface albedo of soils ranges from high to low, and vegetation-covered surfaces and oceans have a low albedo. The Earth's planetary albedo varies mainly through varying cloudiness, snow, ice, leaf area, and land cover changes.

Albedo feedback
Climate feedback involving changes in the Earth's albedo. It usually refers to changes in the cryosphere, which has an albedo much larger (~0.8) than the average planetary albedo (~0.3). In a warming climate, it is anticipated that the cryosphere would shrink, and the Earth's overall albedo would decrease resulting in more solar radiation being absorbed and warming the Earth still further.

Altimeter satellite
Device to measure the time that it takes for a radar pulse to travel from the satellite antenna to the surface and back to the satellite receiver. Combined with precise satellite location data, altimetry measurements can provide sea surface heights.

Anthropogenic
Resulting from or produced by human beings.

Aragonite
Calcium carbonate (limestone) mineral, used by shell- or skeleton-forming, calcifying organisms such as corals, some macro algae, pteropods (marine snails) and non-pteropod molluscs such as bivalves (e.g., clams, oysters), cephalopods (e.g., squids, octopuses). Aragonite is more sensitive to ocean acidification than calcite, also used by many marine organisms. See also Calcification and Ocean acidification.

Arctic oscillation
An atmospheric circulation pattern in which the atmospheric pressure over the polar regions varies on timescales ranging from weeks to decades. The oscillation extends through the depth of the troposphere. From January through March, the Arctic Oscillation also referred to as the North Atlantic Oscillation, extends upward into the stratosphere where it modulates the strength of the westerly vortex that encircles the Arctic polar cap region.

Arthropods
Any of numerous invertebrate animals of the phylum Arthropoda, characterized by an exoskeleton (hard shell). Arthropods include the insects, crustaceans, arachnids, myriapods, and extinct trilobites, and are the largest phylum in the animal kingdom.

Atmosphere
Gaseous envelope surrounding the Earth. The dry atmosphere consists almost entirely of nitrogen and oxygen, together with trace gases such as carbon dioxide and ozone.

Biochar
A type of charcoal resulting from the process of heating organic material in the absence of oxygen (pyrolysis).

Biodiversity
The variability among living organisms from all sources such as terrestrial, marine and other aquatic ecosystems and the ecological complexes of which they are part. It encompasses diversity within species, between species and of ecosystems.

Biophysics (also biological physics)
An interdisciplinary science that employs and develops theories and methods of the physical sciences for the investigation of biological systems. Studies included under the umbrella of biophysics span all levels of biological organization, from the molecular scale to whole organisms and ecosystems. Biophysics is closely related to biochemistry, nanotechnology, bioengineering, agrophysics and systems biology.

Calcification
The process in which the mineral calcium builds up in soft tissue, causing it to harden. Calcification can be used for classification purposes based on the mineral balance and the location of the calcification.

Calcium carbonate ($CaCO_3$)
Chemical compound found as rock in all parts of the world and the main component of seashells and the shell of snails. Calcium carbonate is the active ingredient in agricultural lime.

Calving
Process by which ice breaks off a glacier's terminus; usually the term is used for tidewater glaciers or glaciers that end in lakes, but can also refer to ice that falls from hanging glaciers.

Carbon dioxide (CO_2)
A naturally occurring gas and a by-product from burning fossil fuels or biomass, land-use changes or industrial processes. It is the principal anthropogenic greenhouse gas that affects Earth's radiative balance.

Carbon sequestration
The process of increasing the carbon content of a reservoir other than the atmosphere (see Carbon sink).

Carbon sink
Pool or reservoir that absorbs or takes up released carbon from another part of the carbon cycle. The 4 sinks are the atmosphere, terrestrial biosphere (usually including freshwater systems), oceans, and sediments.

Carbonate (CO_3)
A salt or ester of carbonic acid. Also used as a verb, to describe carbonation (to carbonate), which is the process of raising the concentrations of carbonate and bicarbonate ions in water to produce carbonated water and other carbonated beverages by adding carbon dioxide.

Catchment
An area that collects and drains rainwater.

Circulation patterns
General geometric configuration of atmospheric circulation usually applied in synoptic meteorology to large-scale features of synoptic charts and mean charts.

Circumpolar circulation
Deep ocean currents that transport deep and intermediate water between the oceans. For example, the Antarctic Circumpolar Current is an important feature of the ocean's deep circulation because it contributes to the deep circulation between the Atlantic, Indian, and Pacific Oceans.

Climate

'Average weather' described in terms of the mean and variability of relevant quantities such as temperature, precipitation and wind over a period of time ranging from months to thousands or millions of years. Climate can also be used to describe the state, including a statistical description, of the climate system. The classical period of time is 30 years, as defined by the World Meteorological Organization (WMO).

Climate change

Alternations in the state of the climate system over time due to natural variability or as a result of human activity. The United Nations Framework Convention on Climate Change (UNFCCC) defines climate change as "a change of climate which is attributed directly or indirectly to human activity that alters the composition of the global atmosphere and which is in addition to natural variability observed over comparable time periods."

Climate threshold

The point at which external forcing of the climate system triggers a significant climatic or environmental event which is considered unalterable, or recoverable only on very long timescales. For example, widespread bleaching of corals or a collapse of oceanic circulation systems as a result of increasing atmospheric concentration of greenhouse gases in the atmosphere.

Climatology

The scientific study of climate conditions averaged over a period of time on a local, regional or global scale to enable understanding of the periodicity, frequency, and trends of patterns. Recorded average climate is used as a standard against which to measure changes due to natural or human-induced factors.

Coral reef

Rock-like limestone structures along ocean coasts (fringing reefs) or on top of shallow, submerged banks or shelves (barrier reefs, atolls), often found in tropical and subtropical oceans.

Coral bleaching

The paling in colour of the coral which occurs if a coral loses its symbiotic, energy-providing organisms.

Coralline algae

A simple non-flowering type of plant. Coralline algae are red algae in the family Corallinaceae of the order Corallinales. These algae are most typically pink, or some other shade of red and some species can be purple, yellow, blue, white or grey-green in colour and found in tropical marine waters all over the world.

Corals

Common name for the Order Scleractinia, all members of which have hard limestone skeletons, and which are divided into reef-building and non-reef-building, or cold- and warm-water corals.

Crustaceans

A large group of arthropods, comprising almost 52,000 known species. They include various familiar animals, such as crabs, lobsters, crayfish, shrimp, krill and barnacles. The majority of them are aquatic, living in either marine or fresh water environments, but a few groups have adapted to life on land, such as terrestrial crabs, terrestrial hermit crabs and woodlice.

Cryosphere

Component of the climate system consisting of all snow, ice, frozen ground and permafrost on and beneath the surface of the Earth and ocean. See also Glacier.

Desertification

Degradation of land in arid, semi-arid and dry sub-humid areas resulting from various factors including human activities and climatic variations. Often used as an example of a threshold beyond which the underpinning ecosystem cannot restore itself, but requires ever-greater external resources for recovery.

Disappearing climate

The complete disappearance of an extant climate. Disappearing climates are projected to be concentrated in tropical montane regions and the poleward portions of continents.

Drought

Prolonged absence or marked deficiency of precipitation that causes a serious hydrological imbalance. Agricultural drought relates to moisture deficits in the topmost one metre or so of soil (the root zone) that affects crops. Meteorological drought is mainly a prolonged deficit of precipitation, and hydrologic drought is related to below-normal stream flow, lake and groundwater levels.

Drunken forests

An area of trees displaced from their normal vertical alignment. Most commonly occurs in northern subarctic taiga forests of black spruce (Picea mariana) when discontinuous permafrost or ice wedges melt away, causing trees to tilt at various angles. Tilted trees may also be caused by frost heaving, and subsequent palsa development, hummocks, earthflows, forested active rock glaciers, landslides, or earthquakes.

Earth System Science

An interdisciplinary field of study of the behaviour of Earth Systems' components, with an emphasis on observing, understanding and predicting global environmental changes involving interactions between land, atmosphere, water, ice, biosphere, societies, technologies and economies.

Ecosystem

A dynamic and complex system of living organisms and their physical environment interacting with each other as a functional unit. The extent of an ecosystem may range from very small spatial scales to the entire Earth.

Ecosystem services

The benefits derived from ecosystems. These include provisioning services such as food and water, regulating services such as flood and disease control, cultural services, such as spiritual, recreational and cultural benefits, and supporting services, such as nutrient cycling, that maintain the conditions for life on Earth. Also referred to as ecosystem goods-and-services.

El Niño Southern Oscillation

Systematic and re-occuring weather patterns of the ocean-atmosphere system in the tropical Pacific having important consequences for weather around the globe.

Endemic species

Species whose natural occurrence is confined to a certain region and whose distribution is relatively limited.

Erosion

Process of gradual destruction or removal and transport of soil and rock by weathering, mass wasting by streams, glaciers, waves, winds and underground water.

Eustatic sea-level rise

See Sea-level rise.

Evapotranspiration

The transport of water into the atmosphere from surfaces, for example from soil evaporation and vegetation transpiration. The process of evapotranspiration is one of the main consumers of solar energy at the Earth's surface. Apart from precipitation, evapotranspiration is one of the most significant components of the water cycle.

Genotype

The specific genetic makeup of an organism.

Geoengineering
Technological options to achieve a deliberate manipulation of the Earth's climate to produce a planetary cooling effect in order to mitigate the impact of global warming from greenhouse gas emissions.

Glacial retreat
Net movement of the glacier terminus upvalley. Retreat results when the glacier is ablating at a rate faster than its movement downvalley. Retreating termini are usually concave in shape.

Glacier
Mass of land ice flowing downhill (by internal deformation and sliding at the base) and constrained by the surrounding topography such as the sides of a valley or surrounding peaks. A glacier is maintained by accumulation of snow at high altitudes, balanced by melting at low altitudes or discharge into the sea.

Glaciologists
Ice experts and specialists in the scientific study of glaciers and their effects on the landscape and our climate.

Global warming
Gradual increase, observed or projected, in global surface temperature, referred to as the global temperature, as one of the consequences of the enhanced greenhouse effect, which is induced by anthropogenic emissions of greenhouse gases into the atmosphere.

Greenhouse gas (GHG)
Gaseous constituents such as water vapour (H_2O), carbon dioxide (CO_2), nitrous oxide (N_2O), methane (CH_4) and ozone (O_3) in the atmosphere. These gases, both natural and anthropogenic, can absorb and emit radiation at specific wavelengths within the spectrum of thermal infrared radiation emitted by the Earth's surface, the atmosphere, and by clouds causing the warming greenhouse effect.

Groundwater
Water beneath the Earth's surface, often between saturated soil and rock, that supplies wells and springs.

Groundwater recharge
The process by which external water is added to the zone of saturation of an aquifer, either directly into a formation or indirectly by way of another formation.

Headwaters
The source of a river or a stream and the place from which the water in the river or stream originates.

Hydrographic event
An incident that alters the state or current of waters in oceans, rivers or lakes.

Hydrology
Scientific study of water which seeks to understand the complex water system of the Earth and help solve water problems.

Ice cap
A dome-shaped ice mass, usually covering a highland area, which is considerably smaller in extent than an ice sheet.

Ice shelf
A floating slab of ice of considerable thickness extending from the coast (usually of great horizontal extent with a level or gently sloping surface), often filling embayments in the coastline of the ice sheets.

Iceberg
A large block of freshwater ice that has broken off from a snow-formed glacier or ice shelf and is floating in open water.

Icefield
Large sheet of ice which covers an area of land or water.

Interglacial stage
Period of warmer climate that separates two glacial periods. Mid-latitude interglacials are identified by a characteristic sequence of vegetation change from tundra to boreal forest and subsequently deciduous forest.

Inter-tidal zone
An area of the foreshore and seabed that is exposed to the air at low tide and submerged at high tide, or the area between tide marks. Also referred to as the littoral zone.

Logarithmic scale
A measurement that uses the logarithm of a physical quantity instead of the quantity itself.

Magnesium calcite
Carbonate mineral and the most stable polymorph of calcium carbonate ($CaCO_3$). Calcite is often the primary constituent of the shells of marine organisms, e.g. plankton (such as coccoliths and planktic foraminifera), the hard parts of red algae, some sponges, brachiopoda, echinoderms, most bryozoa, and parts of the shells of some bivalves, such as oysters and rudists.

Mangroves
Shrubs and trees of the families Rhizophoraceae, Acanthaceae, Lythraceae, and Arecaceae (palm) or the subfamily Pellicieraceae (family Tetrameristaceae) that grow in dense thickets or forests along tidal estuaries, in salt marshes, and on muddy coasts.

Mega drought
Long drawn out, pervasive and prolonged absence or marked deficiency of precipitation that causes a serious hydrological imbalance lasting much longer than normal, usually a decade or more.

Mesoscale convective system
Cluster of thunderstorms which becomes organized on a scale larger than the individual thunderstorms, and normally persists for several hours or more. Mesoscale convective systems may be round or linear in shape, and include other systems such as tropical cyclones.

Mitigation
A human intervention to reduce the sources or enhance the sinks of greenhouse gases.

Moraine
Glacially formed accumulation of unconsolidated glacial debris (soil and rock) which can occur in currently glaciated and formerly glaciated regions. Moraines may be composed of debris ranging in size from silt-like glacial flour to large boulders. The debris is typically sub-angular to rounded in shape. Moraines may be on the surface of a glacier or deposited as piles or sheets of debris where the glacier has melted. Moraines may also occur when glacier- or iceberg-transported rocks fall into the sea as the ice melts.

Novel climate
Future climate lacking a modern analogue, characterized by high seasonality of temperature, warmer than any present climate globally, with spatially variable shifts in precipitation, and increase in the risk of species reshuffling into future no-analog communities. Novel climates are projected to develop primarily in the tropics and subtropics.

Ocean acidification
A decrease in the pH of seawater due to the uptake of anthropogenic carbon dioxide.

Oceanography
Scientific study of the oceans using science and mathematics to explain the complex interactions between seawater, fresh water, polar ice caps, the atmosphere and the biosphere.

Outburst floods
An incident taking place when a lake contained by a glacier bursts. Floods happen due to erosion, a build-up of water pressure, an avalanche of rock or heavy snow, an earthquake or cryoseism, volcanic eruptions under the ice, or if a large enough portion of a glacier breaks off and massively displaces the waters in a glacial lake at its base.

Outlet glaciers
A stream of ice from an ice cap to the sea.

Oxygen isotope ratio
Cyclical variations in the ratio of the mass of oxygen with an atomic weight of 18 to the mass of oxygen with an atomic weight of 16 present in some substances, such as polar ice or calcite in ocean core samples. The ratio is linked to water temperature of ancient oceans, which in turn reflects ancient climates. Cycles in the ratio mirror climate changes in geologic history.

Ozone (O_3)
A gaseous atmospheric constituent created naturally and by photochemical reactions involving gases resulting from human activities (e.g. smog) in the troposphere. Tropospheric ozone acts as a greenhouse gas. In the stratosphere, it is created by the interaction between solar ultraviolet radiation and molecular oxygen (O_2). Stratospheric ozone plays a dominant role in the stratospheric radiative balance. Its concentration is highest in the ozone layer.

Permafrost
The surface layer of soil, sediment and rock that remains at or below 0 degrees Celsius for at least two consecutive years.

Photosynthesis
The process by which plants take carbon dioxide from the air (or bicarbonate in water) to build carbohydrates, releasing oxygen in the process. There are several pathways of photosynthesis with different responses to atmospheric CO_2 concentrations.

Pyrolysis
A thermal decomposition process of organic material at high temperature in the absence of oxygen.

Radiative forcing
The change in the net, downward minus upward, irradiance (expressed in W m−2) at the tropopause due to a change in an external driver of climate change, for example, a change in the concentration of carbon dioxide or the output of the Sun. Radiative forcing is computed with all tropospheric properties held fixed at their unperturbed values, and after allowing for stratospheric temperatures, if perturbed, to readjust to radiative-dynamical equilibrium.

Savanna
Tropical or sub-tropical grassland or woodland biomes with scattered shrubs, individual trees or a very open canopy of trees, all characterized by a dry (arid, semi-arid or semi-humid) climate.

Salinity
The presence of soluble salts in soils or waters such as sodium chloride, magnesium and calcium sulfates and bicarbonates. It usually results from water tables rising to, or close to, the ground surface.

Sea-level rise
Increase in the mean level of the ocean. Eustatic sea-level rise is a change in global average sea level brought about by an increase in the volume of the world ocean. Relative sea-level rise occurs where there is a local increase in the level of the ocean relative to the land, which might be due to ocean rise and/or land level subsidence. In areas subject to rapid land-level uplift, relative sea level can fall.

Sediment respiration
Process whereby living organisms convert organic matter to carbon dioxide and methane, releasing energy and consuming molecular oxygen.

Small ice cap instability
Behaviour of ice lines caused by variations in temperature, gradient, and amplitude of the seasonal cycle affecting the strength of the albedo feedback. Small ice cap instability may be a possible mechanism for the formation of the Antarctic ice sheet.

Stratosphere
The highly stratified region of the atmosphere above the troposphere extending from about 10 km (ranging from 9 km at high latitudes to 16 km in the tropics on average) to about 50 km altitude.

Symbiotic relationship
A close ecological relationship between the individuals of two or more different species. Sometimes a symbiotic relationship benefits both species, sometimes one species benefits at the other's expense, and in other cases neither species benefits.

Talik
An unfrozen section of ground found above, below, or within a layer of discontinuous permafrost. These layers can also be found beneath water bodies in a layer of continuous permafrost.

Terrestrial ecosystems
A community of organisms and their environment that occurs on the landmasses of continents and islands.

Thermal expansion
An increase in volume (and decrease in density) that results from warming water. For example, warming of the ocean leads to an expansion of the ocean volume and hence an increase in sea level.

Thermodynamic equilibrium
A condition in a system where the distribution of mass and energy moves towards maximum entropy.

Thermohaline convection (THC)
Large-scale, density-driven circulation in the ocean, caused by differences in temperature and salinity. In the North Atlantic, the thermohaline circulation consists of warm surface water flowing northward and cold deepwater flowing southward, resulting in a net poleward transport of heat. The surface water sinks in highly restricted regions located in high latitudes. Also called Meridional Overturning Circulation (MOC).

Threshold
The level of magnitude of a system process at which sudden or rapid change occurs. A point or level at which new properties emerge in an ecological, economic or other system, invalidating predictions based on mathematical relationships that apply at lower levels.

Topography
The relief and shape exhibited by a surface.

Tsunami
A large wave produced by a submarine earthquake, landslide or volcanic eruption.

Westerlies
Dominant winds of the mid-latitudes. These winds move from the subtropical highs to the subpolar lows from west to east.

Wetland
The transitional, regularly waterlogged area of poorly drained soils, often between an aquatic and a terrestrial ecosystem, fed from rain, surface water or groundwater. Wetlands are characterized by a prevalence of vegetation adapted for life in saturated soil conditions.

Source: UNEP 2007, IPCC 2007a, IPCC 2007b, IPCC 2007c, MA 2005

Acronyms and Abbreviations

ACC	Antarctic Circumpolar Current
AGRA	Alliance for a Green Revolution in Africa
AMS	American Meteorological Society
AR4	Fourth Assessment Report
AWC	Advanced Wood Combustion
BAS	British Antarctic Survey
Ca	Calcium
CAA	Canadian Arctic Archipelago
$CaCO_3$	Calcium carbonate
CCS	Carbon Capture and Storage
CDR	Carbon Dioxide Removal
CCSP	Climate Change Science Program
CDIAC	Carbon Dioxide Information Analysis Centre
CH_4	Methane
CO_2	Carbon dioxide
CO_3	Carbonate
CO_3^{-2}	Carbonate ion
CSIRO	Commonwealth Scientific and Industrial Research Organisation
DAMOCLES	Developing Arctic Modeling and Observing Capabilities for Long-term Environmental Studies
DSWC	Dense Shelf Water Cascades
ENSO	El Niño Southern Oscillation
ERHIN	Estudio de los Recursos Hídricos procedentes de la Innivación
ESA	European Space Agency
FAO	Food and Agriculture Organization
FYI	First Year Ice
GCOS	Global Climate Observing System
GHG	Greenhouse gas
GISS	Goddard Institute for Space Studies
GMT	Global Mean Temperature
GRACE	Gravity Recovery and Climate Experiment
GTOS	Global Terrestrial Observing System
H^+	Hydrogen
H_2CO_3	Carbonic acid
H_2O	Water
HCO_3^{-1}	Bicarbonate ion
IAASTD	International Assessment of Agricultural Knowledge, Science and Technology for Development
ICIMOD	International Centre for Integrated Mountain Development
IEA	International Energy Agency
IGBP	International Geosphere-Biosphere Programme
IGY	International Geophysical Year
IMO	International Maritime Organization
IPCC	Intergovernmental Panel on Climate Change
IPCC AR4	Intergovernmental Panel on Climate Change, The Fourth Assessment Report
IPCC AR5	Intergovernmental Panel on Climate Change, The Fifth Assessment Report
IPCC WG2	Intergovernmental Panel on Climate Change, Working Group 2
IPY	International Polar Year
masl	Metres above sea level
mm	Millimetre
MOC	Meridional Overturning Circulation
MPA	Marine Protected Areas
MYI	Multi Year Ice
N_2O	Nitrous oxide
NAM	Northern Annular Mode
NASA	National Aeronautics and Space Administration
NASA/JPL	National Aeronautics and Space Administration/Jet Propulsion Laboratory
NASA/GSFC	National Aeronautics and Space Administration / Goddard Space Flight Center
NOAA	National Oceanic and Atmospheric Administration
NOAA-ESRL	National Oceanic and Atmospheric Administration-Earth System Research Laboratory
NPI	Norwegian Polar Institute
NSIDC	National Snow and Ice Data Center
Pg	10^{15} grams, Billion tonnes
ppm	parts per million
REDD	Reducing Emissions from Deforestation and Forest Degradation
SCOPE	Scientific Committee on Problems of the Environment
SEG	Scientific Expert Group
SIO	Scripps Institution of Oceanography
SLR	Sea-level rise
SMD	Seasonal Melt Departure
SO_2	Sulphur dioxide
SRM	Solar Radiation Management
SST	Sea surface temperature
TAR	Third Assessment Report
THC	Thermohaline circulation
UN	United Nations
UNEP	United Nations Environment Programme
UNFCCC	United Nations Framework Convention on Climate Change
USGS	United States Geological Survey
WCMC	World Conservation Monitoring Centre
WCRP	World Climate Research Programme
WGMS	World Glacier Monitoring Service

References

AGRA (2008). Revitalising Small-Scale Farming Across Africa. Alliance for a Green Revolution in Africa, 2008. http://www.agra-alliance.org/

Al-Juaied, M. and Whitmore, A. (2009). Realistic costs of carbon capture Discussion Paper 2009-08, Energy Technology Innovation Research Group, Belfer Center for Science and International Affairs, Harvard Kennedy School, July 2009

Allan, R.P. and Soden, B.J. (2008). Atmospheric Warming and the Amplification of Precipitation Extremes. *Science* 321(5895): 1481-1484

Allen, S.E. and Durrieu de Madron, X. (2009). A review of the role of submarine canyons in deep-ocean exchange with the shelf. *Ocean Science Discuss.* 6, 1369–1406

Alley, R.B. (2007). Wally Was Right: Predictive Ability of the North Atlantic "Conveyor Belt" Hypothesis for Abrupt Climate Change. *Annual Review of Earth and Planetary Sciences* 35, 241-272

Alley, R.B., Marotzke, J., Nordhaus, W.D., Overpeck, J.T., Peteet, D.M., Pielke Jr., R.A., Pierrehumbert, R.T., Rhines, P.B., Stocker, T.F., Talley, L.D. and Wallace, J.M. (2003). Abrupt Climate Change. *Science* 299(5615), 2005-2010

Alongi, M.D. (2008). Mangrove forests: Resilience, protection from tsunamis, and responses to global climate change. *Estuarine, Coastal and Shelf Science* 76, 1-13

Anderson, R.F., Ali, S., Bradtmiller, L.I., Nielse, S.H.H., Fleisher, M.Q., Anderson, B.E. and Burckle, L.H. (2009). Wind-Driven Upwelling in the Southern Ocean and the Deglacial Rise in Atmospheric CO_2. *Science* 323(5920), 1443-1448

Anthoff, D., Nicholls, R.J., Tol, R.S.J. and Vafeidis, A.T. (2006). Global and regional exposure to large rises in sea-level: a sensitivity analysis. Working Paper 96. Tyndall Centre for Climate Change Research, Norwich

Archer, D. (2007). Methane hydrate stability and anthropogenic climate change. *Biogeoscience* 4, 521-44

Arendt, A., Luthcke, S. B., and Hock R. (2009). GRACE Mascon Estimates of Glacier Changes in the St. Elias Mountains: Can Mass Balance Models Explain Recent Trends? *Annals of Glaciology*, 50(50), 148-154

Aumann, H.H., Ruzmaikin, A. and Teixeira, J. (2008). Frequency of severe storms and global warming. *Geophysical Research Letters* 35, L19805

Bahr, D.B., Dyurgerov, M. and Meier, M.F. (2009). Sea-level rise from glaciers and ice caps: A lower bound. *Geophysical Research Letters* 10.1029

Baker, A.C., Glynn, P.W. and Riegl, B. (2008). Climate change and coral reef bleaching: An ecological assessment of long-term impacts, recovery trends and future outlook. *Estuarine, Coastal and Shelf Science* 80(4), 435-471

Baker, V.R. (1998). Catastrophism and uniformitarianism: logical roots and current relevance in geology. *Geological Society, London, Special Publications* 143, 171-182

Bamber, J.L., Riva, R.E.M., Vermeersen, B.L.A. and LeBrocq, A.M. (2009). Reassessment of the Potential Sea-Level Rise from a Collapse of the West Antarctic Ice Sheet. *Science* 324, 901-903

Barnett, T. P., Pierce, D.W., Hidalgo, H.G., Bonfils, C., Santer, B.D., Das, T., Bala, G., Wood, A.W., Nozawa, T. and Mirin, A.A. (2008). Human-Induced Changes in the Hydrology of the Western United States. *Science* 319, 1080-1083

BAS (2008). *Antarctic ice shelf 'hangs by a thread'*. British Antarctic Survey http://www.antarctica.ac.uk/press/press_releases/press_release.php?id=376

Baskett, M.L., Gaines, S.D. and Nisbet, R.M. (2009). Symbiont diversity may help coral reefs survive moderate climate change. *Ecological Applications* 19(1), 3-17

Beaugrand, G., Pheluzack, C. and Edwards, M. (2009). Rapid biogeographical plankton shifts in the North Atlantic Ocean. *Global Change Biology* 15, 1790-1803

Benn, D.I., Warren, C.R. and Mottram, R.H. (2007). Calving processes and the dynamics of calving glaciers. *Earth Science Review* 82, 143-179

Betts, R., Sanderson, M. and Woodward, S. (2008). Effects of large-scale Amazon forest degradation on climate and air quality through fluxes of carbon dioxide, water, energy, mineral dust and isoprene. *Philosophical Transactions of the Royal Society B*, 363(1498), 1873-1880

Blackford, J., Jones, N., Proctor, R., Holt, J., Widdicombe, S., Lowe, D. and Rees, A. (2009). An initial assessment of the potential environmental impact of CO_2 escape from marine carbon capture and storage systems. *Proceedings of the Institution of Mechanical Engineers, Part A: Journal of Power and Energy* 223(3), 269-280

Blackstock, J.J., Battisti, D.S., Caldeira, K., Eardley, D.M., Katz, J.I., Keith, D.W., Patrinos, A.A.N., Schrag, D.P., Socolow, R.H. and Koonin, S.E. (2009). *Climate Engineering Responses to Climate Emergencies*. Novim, archived online at http://arxiv.org/pdf/0907.5140

Boé, J., Terray, L., Cassou, C. and Najac, J. (2009). Uncertainties in European summer precipitation changes: role of large scale circulation. *Climate Dynamics* 33, 265-276

Bonan, G.B. (2008). Forests and Climate Change: Forcing, Feedbacks, and the Climate Benefits of Forests. *Science* 320, 1444-1449

Böning, C.W., Dispert, A., Visbeck, M., Rintoul, S.R. and Schwarzkopf, F.U. (2008). The response of the Antarctic Circumpolar Current to recent climate change. *Nature Geoscience* 1, 864-869

Bosire, J.O., Dahdouh-Guebas, F., Walton, M., Crona, B.I., Lewis III, R.R., Field, C., Kairo, J.G. and Koedam, N. (2008). Functionality of restored mangroves: A review. *Aquatic Botany* 89(2), 251-259

Box, J.E., Yang, L., Bromwich, D.H. and Bai, L.S. (2009). Greenland ice sheet surface air temperature variability: 1840-2007. *Journal of Climate* 22(14), 4029-4049

Boyd, P.W. (2008). Ranking geo-engineering schemes. *Nature Geoscience* 1, 722-724

Braithwaite, R.J. (2009). Calculation of sensible-heat flux over a melting ice surface using simple climate data and daily measurements of ablation. *Annals of Glaciology* 50(50), 9-15

Braun, M., Humbert, A. and Moll, A. (2008). Changes of Wilkins Ice Shelf over the past 15 years and inferences on its stability. *The Cryosphere* 2, 341-382

Brewer, P.G., and Peltzer, E.T. (2009). Limits to Marine Life. *Science* 324(5925), 347-348

Briner, J.P., Bini, A.C. and Anderson, R.S. (2009). Rapid early Holocene retreat of a Laurentide outlet glacier through an Arctic fjord. *Nature Geoscience* 2, 496-499

Broecker, W.S., Kennett, J.P., Flower, B.P., Teller, J.T., Trumbore, S., Bonani, G. and Wolfli, W. (1989). Routing Of Meltwater From The Laurentide Ice Sheet During The Younger Dryas Cold Episode. *Nature* 341, 318-321

Brovkin, V. and Claussen, M. (2008). Climate-Driven Ecosystem Succession in the Sahara: The Past 6000 Years. *Science* 322, 1326 DOI: 10.1126/science.1163381

Brovkin, V., Raddatz, T., Reick, C.H., Claussen, M. and Gayler, V. (2009). Global biogeophysical interactions between forest and climate. *Geophysical Research Letters* 36, L07405

Brown, B. (2007). Resilience Thinking Applied to the Mangroves of Indonesia. IUCN and Mangrove Action Project, Yogyakarta, Indonesia

Bruun, S., El-Zahery, T. and Jensen, L. (2009). Carbon sequestration with biochar – stability and effect on decomposition of soil organic matter. *IOP Conference Series: Earth and Environmental Science* 6, 242010

Bryden, H.L., Longworth, H.R. and Cunningham, S.A. (2005). Slowing of the Atlantic meridional overturning circulation at 25° N. *Nature* 438, 655-657

Burgents J. E., Burnett K. G. and Burnett L. E. (2005) Effects of hypoxia and hypercapnic hypoxia on the localization and the elimination of Vibrio campbelli in Litopenaeus vannamei, the Pacific white shrimp. *Biological Bulletin* 208, 159–68

Burgess, D.O. and Sharp, M.J. (2008). Recent changes in thickness of the Devon Island ice cap, Canada. *Journal of Geophysical Research* (Solid Earth) 113, B07204

CAFF (2001). Arctic Flora and Fauna: Status and Conservation. Conservation of Arctic Flora and Fauna. Helsinki, Edita

Caldeira, K. (2009). Ocean acidification: humanity and the environment in geologic time. *IOP Conference Series: Earth and Environmental Science* 6, 462004

Caldeira K. and Wickett M. E. (2003). Anthropogenic carbon and ocean pH. *Nature* 425, 365

Canadell, J.G. and Raupach, M.R. (2008). Managing Forests for Climate Change Mitigation. *Science* 320, 1456-1457

Canadell, J.G. and Raupach, M.R. (2009). Vulnerabilities associated with the Arctic terrestrial carbon cycle. *In*: Arctic Climate Feedbacks: Global Implications, Sommerkorn M., Hassol S.J. World Wildlife Fund

Canadell, J.G., Le Quéré, C., Raupach, M.R., Field, C.B., Buitenhuis, E.T., Ciais, P., Conway, T.J., Gillett, N.P., Houghton, R.A., and Marland, G. (2007). Contributions to accelerating atmospheric CO_2 growth from economic activity, carbon intensity, and efficiency of natural sinks. *Proceedings of the National Academy of Sciences* 104(47), 18866-18870

Cao, L. and Caldeira, K. (2008). Atmospheric CO_2 stabilization and ocean acidification. *Geophysical Research Letters* 35, L19609

Cazenave, A. and Nerem, R.S. (2004). Present-day sea level change: Observations and causes. *Review of Geophysics* 42, RG3001

Cazenave, A., Dominh, K., Guinehut, S., Berthier, E., Llovel, W., Ramillien, G, Ablain, M. and Larnicol, G. (2009). Sea level budget over 2003–2008: A reevaluation from GRACE space gravimetry, satellite altimetry and Argo, *Global and Planetary Change* 65, 83-88

Ceccon, E. and Miramontes, O. (2008). Reversing deforestation? Bioenergy and society in two Brazilian models. *Ecological Economics* 67, 311-317

Chapin III, F.S., Randerson, J.T., McGuire, A.D., Foley, J.A. and Field, C.B. (2008). Changing feedbacks in the climate-biosphere system. *Frontiers in the Ecology and Environment* 6(6), 313-320

Chatenoux, B. and Peduzzi, P. (2007). Impacts of the 2004 Indian Ocean tsunami: analysing the potential protecting role of environmental features. *Natural Hazards* 40(2), 289-304

Chaudhary, P. and Aryal, K.P. (2009). Global Warming in Nepal: Challenges and Policy. *Journal of Forest and Livelihood* 8(1), 4-13

Chazal, J. and Rounsevell, M.D.A. (2009). Land-use and climate change within assessments of biodiversity change: A review. *Global Environmental Change* 19, 306-315

Cheung, W.W.L., Close, C., Lam, V., Sarmiento, J.L., Watson, R. and Pauly, D. (2008). Application of macroecological theory to predict effects of climate change on global fisheries potential. *Marine Ecology Progress Series* 365, 187-193

Cheung, W.W.L., Lam, V.W.Y., Sarmiento, J.L., Kearney, K., Watson, R. and Pauly, D. (2009). Projecting global marine biodiversity impacts under climate change scenarios. *Fish and Fisheries* 10(3), 235-251

Church, J. (2008). Sea-level rise and global climate change. World Climate Research Programme (WCRP) News. http://wcrp.wmo.int/documents/WCRPnews_20080221.pdf

Church, J.A., White, N.J., Aarup, T., Wilson, W.S., Woodworth, P.L., Domingues, C.M., Hunter, J.R. and Lambeck, K. (2008). Understanding global sea levels: past, present and future. *Sustainability Science* 3(1), 9-22

Clark, P.U., Pisias, N.G., Stocker, T.F. and Weaver, A.J. (2002). The role of the thermohaline circulation in abrupt climate change. *Nature* 415, 863-869

Clark, P.U. and Weaver, A.J. Coordinating Lead Authors (2008). Abrupt Climate Change: U.S. Climate Change Research Program, Synthesis and Assessment Product 3.4, 459p

Clement, J., Vercauteren, J., Verstraeten, W.W., Ducoffre, G., Barrios, J.M., Van-damme, A-M., Maes, P. and Van Ranst, M. (2009). Relating increasing hantavirus incidences to the changing climate: the mast connection. *International Journal of Health Geographics* 8,1

Colwell, R.K., Brehm, G., Cardelús, C.L. Gilman, A.C. and Longino, J.T. (2008). Global Warming, Elevational Range Shifts, and Lowland Biotic Attrition in the Wet Tropics. *Science* 322(5899), 258-261

Comiso, J.C., Parkinson, C.L., Gersten, R. and Stock, L. (2008). Accelerated decline in the Arctic sea ice cover. *Geophysical Research Letters* 35, L01703

Cook, K.H. (2008). The mysteries of Sahel droughts. *Nature Geoscience* 1(10), 647-648

Cooley, S.R. and Doney, S.C. (2009). Anticipating ocean acidification's economic consequences for commercial fisheries. *Environmental Research Letters* 4(2) doi:10.1088/1748-9326/

Costello, A., Abbas, M., Allen, A., Ball, S., Bell, S., Bellamy, R., Friel, S., Groce, N., Johnson, A., Kett, M., Lee, M., Levy, C., Maslin, M., McCoy, D., McGuire, B., Montgomery, H., Napier, D., Pagel, C., Patel, J., de Oliveira, J.A.P., Redclift, N., Rees, H., Rogger, D., Scott, J., Stephenson, J., Twigg, J., Wolff, J. and Patterson, C. (2009). Managing the health effects of climate change. *The Lancet* 373(9676), 1693-1733

Cox, P.M., Harris, P.P., Huntingford, C., Betts, R.A., Collins, M., Jones, C.D., Jupp, T.E., Marengo, J.A. and Nobre, C.A. (2008). Increasing risk of Amazonian drought due to decreasing aerosol pollution. *Nature* 453(7192), 212-215

Craft, C., Clough, J., Ehman, J., Joye, S., Park, R., Pennings, S., Guo, H. and Machmuller, M. (2009). Forecasting the effects of accelerated sea-level rise on tidal marsh ecosystem services. *Frontiers in Ecology and the Environment* 7(2), 73-78

Currano, E.D., Wilf, P., Wing, S. L., Labandeira, C.C., Lovelock, E.C. and Royer, D.L. (2008). Sharply increased insect herbivory during the Paleocene-Eocene Thermal Maximum. *Proceedings of the National Academy of Sciences* 105, 1960-1964

Dakos, V., Scheffer, M., Van Nes, E.H., Brovkin, V., Petoukhov, V. and Held, H. (2008). Slowing down as an early warning signal for abrupt climate change. *Proceedings of the National Academy of Sciences* 105(38), 14308-14312

Das, S.B., Joughin, I., Behn, M.D., Howat, I.M., King, M.A., Lizarralde, D. and Bhatia, M.P. (2008). Fracture Propagation to the Base of the Greenland Ice Sheet During Supraglacial Lake Drainage. *Science* 320(5877), 778-781

DeLucia, E.H., Casteel, C.L., Nabity, P.D. and O'Neill, B.F. (2008). Insects take a bigger bite out of plants in a warmer, higher carbon dioxide world. *Proceedings of the National Academy of Sciences* 105(6), 1781-1782

Delworth, T.L., Rosati, A., Stouffer, R.J., Dixon, K.W., Dunne, J., Findell, K.L., Ginoux, P., Gnanadesikan, A., Gordon, C.T., Griffies, S.M., Gudgel, R., Harrison, M.J., Held, I.M., Hemler, R.S., Horowitz, L.W., Klein, S.A., Knutson, T.R., Lin, S., Ramaswamy, V., Schwarzkopf, M.D., Sirutis, J.J., Spelman, M.J., Stern, W.F., Winton, M., Wittenberg, A.T. and Wyman, B. (2006). GFDL's CM2 global coupled climate models. Part I: Formulation and simulation characteristics. *Journal of Climate* 19(5), 643–674

Delworth, T.L., Clark, P.U., Holland, M., Johns, W.E., Kuhlbrodt, T., Lynch-Stieglitz, J., Morrill, C., Seager, R. and Weaver, A.J. (2008). The potential for abrupt change in the Atlantic Meridional Overturning Circulation. Abrupt Climate Change, U.S. Climate Change Research Program, Synthesis and Assessment Product 3.4.

Denman, K.L., Brasseur, G., Chidthaisong, A., Ciais, P., Cox, P.M., Dickinson, R.E., Hauglustaine, D., Heinze, C., Holland, E., Jacob, D., Lohmann, U., Ramachandran, S., da Silva Dias, P.L., Wofsy, S.C., and Zhang, X. (2007). *Couplings Between Changes in the Climate System and Biogeochemistry.* In: *Climate Change 2007: The Physical Science Basis.* Contribution of Working Group I to the Fourth Assessment Report of the Intergovernmental Panel on Climate Change [Solomon, S., D. Qin, M. Manning, Z. Chen, M. Marquis, K.B. Averyt, M.Tignor and H.L. Miller (eds.)]. Cambridge University Press, Cambridge, United Kingdom and New York, NY, USA.

Denny, M.W., Hunt, L.J.H., Miller, L.P. and Harley, C.D.G. (2009). On the prediction of extreme ecological events. *Ecological Monographs* 79(3), 397-421

Deutsch, C.A., Tewksbury, J.J., Huey, R.B., Sheldon, K.S., Ghalambor, C.K., Haak, D.C. and Martin, P.R. (2008). Impacts of climate warming on terrestrial ectotherms across latitude. *Proceedings of the National Academy of Sciences* 105(18), 6668-6672

Dietz, H. and Edwards, P.J. (2006). Recognition of changing processes during plant invasions may help reconcile conflicting evidence of the causes. *Ecology* 87, 1359-1367

Diffenbaugh, N. S., Pal, J. S., Giorgi, F. and Gao, X. (2007). Heat stress intensification in the Mediterranean climate change hotspot, *Geophysical Reseach Letters* 34, L11706

Diouf, J. (2008). FAO Reform: Director-General Diouf Calls for New World Agricultural Order. Food and Agricultural Organization of the United Nations Press Release, November 19, 2008

Dmitrenko, I., Polyakov, I.V., Kirillov, S., Timokhov, L., Frolov, I.E., Sokolov, V.T., Simmons, H.L., Ivanov, V.V. and Walsh, D. (2008). Towards A Warmer Arctic Ocean: Spreading Of The Early 21st Century Atlantic Water Warm Anomaly Along The Eurasian Basin Margins. *Journal of Geophysical Research* 113, C05023

Doherty, S.J., Bojinski, S., Henderson-Sellers, A., Noone, K., Goodrich, D., Bindoff, N.L., Church, J.A., Hibbard, K.A., Karl, T.R., Kajfez-Bogataj, L., Lynch, A.H., Parker, D.E., Prentice, I.C., Ramaswamy, V., Saunders, R.W., Smith, S.M., Steffen, K., Stocker, T.F., Thorne, P.W., Trenberth, K.E., Verstraete, M.M. and Zwiers, F.W. (2009). Lessons Learned from IPCC AR4: Scientific Developments Needed to Understand, Predict, and Respond To Climate Change. *American Meteorological Society* 90(4), 497-513

Domingues, C.M., Church, J.A., White, N.J., Gleckler, P.J., Wijffels, S.E., Barker, P.M. and Dunn, J.R. (2008). Improved estimates of upper-ocean warming and multi-decadal sea-level rise. *Nature* 453, 1090-1093

Doney, S.C. and Schimel, D.S. (2007). Carbon and climate system coupling on timescales from the Precambrian to the Anthropocene. *Annual Reviews of Environment and Resources* 32, 31-66

Doney, S.C., Fabry, V.J., Feely, R.A. and Kleypas, J.A. (2009). Ocean Acidification: The Other CO_2 Problem. *Annual Review of Marine Science* 1, 169-192

Donner, S.D., Knutson, T.R. and Oppenheimer, M. (2007). Model-based assessment of the role of human-induced climate change in the 2005 Caribbean coral bleaching event. *Proceedings of the National Academy of Sciences* 104(13), 5483-5488

Dossani, S. (2008). Human Need and Corporate Greed, Understanding the Call for a New Green Revolution in Africa. Africa Action Special Guest Paper Series, Africa Action, August 2008

Dowdeswell, J.A., Benham, T.J., Strozzi, T. and Hagen, J.O., (2008). Iceberg calving flux and mass balance of the Austfonna ice cap on Nordaustlandet, Svalbard. *Journal of Geophysical Research* 113,

Dulvy, N.K., Rogers, S.I., Jennings, S., Vanessa, S., Dye, S.R., and Skjoldal, H.R. (2008). Climate change and deepening of the North Sea fish assemblage: a biotic indicator of warming seas. *Journal of Applied Ecology* 45, 1029-1039

Dutton, A., Bard, E., Antonioli, F., Esat, T.M., Lambeck, K. and McCulloch, M.T. (2009). Phasing and amplitude of sea-level and climate change during the penultimate interglacial. *Nature Geoscience* 2, 355-359

Earth System Science Partnership (2001). Challenges of a Changing Earth, Global Change Open Scientific Conference. Amsterdam, The Netherlands, 13 July 2001

Eby, M., Zickfeld, K., Montenegro, A., Archer, D., Meissner, K.J. and Weaver, A.J. (2009). Lifetime of Anthropogenic Climate Change: Millennial Time Scales of Potential CO_2 and Surface Temperature Perturbations. *Journal of Climate* 22(10), 2501-2511

Eggermont, H., Russell, J. and Verschuren, D. (2007). Response of Rwenzori (Uganda – DR Congo) Glaciers and Mountain Lake Ecosystems to Climate Change: Past, Present, Future. *American Geophysical Union, Fall Meeting*. Abstract GC32A-07

Eisenman, I. and Wettlaufer, J.S. (2009). Nonlinear threshold behavior during the loss of Arctic sea ice. *Proceedings of the National Academy of Sciences* 106, 28-32

Eldrett, J.S., Greenwood, D.R., Harding, I.C. and Huber, M. (2009). Increased seasonality through the Eocene to Oligocene transition in northern high latitudes. *Nature* 459, 969-973

Elsner, J.B., Kossin, J.P and Jagger, T.H. (2008). The increasing intensity of the strongest tropical cyclones. *Nature* 455, 92-95

Elzen, M. and Höhne, N. (2008). Reductions of greenhouse gas emissions in Annex I and non-Annex I countries for meeting concentration stabilisation targets. *Climatic Change* 91, 249–274

England, J.H., Lakeman, T.R., Lemmen, D.S., Bednarski, J.M., Stewart, T.G. and Evans, D.J.A. (2008). A millennial-scale record of Arctic Ocean sea ice variability and the demise of the Ellesmere Island ice shelves. *Geophysical Research Letters* 35, L19502

ERHIN (2009). Datos sobre la nieve y los glaciares en las cordilleras españolas. El programa ERHIN (1984-2008).

Eriksson, E., Gillespie, A.R., Gustavsson, L., Langvall, O., Olsson, M., Sathre, R. and Stendahl, J. (2007). Integrated carbon analysis of forest management practices and wood substitution. *Canadian Journal of Forest Research* 37(3), 671-681

ESA (2007). Satellites witness lowest Arctic ice coverage in history. European Space Agency. http://www.esa.int/esaCP/SEMYTC13J6F_index_1.html

ESA (2009). Collapse of the ice bridge supporting Wilkins Ice Shelf appears imminent. European Space Agency. http://www.esa.int/esaCP/SEMD07EH1TF_index_0.html html

Fabry, V.J., Seibel, B.A., Feely, R.A. and Orr, J.C. (2008). Impacts of ocean acidification on marine fauna and ecosystem processes. *ICES Journal of Marine Science* 65, 414-432

Fagre, D.B., Charles, C.W., Allen, C.D., Birkeland, C., Chapin III, F.S., Groffman, P.M., Guntenspergen, G.R., Knapp, A.K., McGuire, A.D., P.J. Mulholland, Peters, D.P.C., Roby, D.D. and Sugihara, G. (2009). Thresholds of climate change in Ecosystems: Final Report, Synthesis and Assessment Product 4.2. U.S. Geological Survey. A report by the U.S. Climate Change Science Program and the Subcommittee on Global Change Research

Fahey, T.J., Woodbury, P.B., Battles, J.J., Goodale, C.L., Hamburg, S., Ollinger, S., Woodall, C.W. (2009). Forest carbon storage: ecology, management, and policy. *Frontiers in Ecology and the Environment* doi:10.1890/080169

FAO (2008). Soaring Food Prices: Perspectives Impacts and Actions Required. Report of High-level Conference on World Food Security: Challenges of Climate Change and Bioenergy 3-5 June, Rome Italy. Food and Agricultural Organization of the United Nations

Feely, R. A., Sabine C. L., Hernandez-Ayon, J. M., Lanson, D. and Hales, B. (2008) Evidence for upwelling of corrosive `acidified' water onto the continental shelf. *Science* 320, 1490–1492

Foden, W., Mace, G., Vié, J-C., Angulo, A., Butchard, S., DeVantier. L., Dublin, H., Gutsche, A., Stuart, S. and Turak, E. (2008). Species susceptibility to climate change impacts. *In*: Vié, J.-C., Hilton-Taylor, C. and Stuart S.N. (eds.) *The 2008 Review of the IUCN Red List of Threatened Species*. IUCN, Gland, Switzerland.

Forster, P. M., Bodeker, G., Schofield, R., Solomon, S., and Thompson, D. (2007). Effects of ozone cooling in the tropical lower stratosphere and upper troposphere. *Geophysical Research Letters* 34, L23813

Fowler, C. (2007). Norway to build 'fail-safe' conservation site on Arctic Archipelago: A publication about agricultural biodiversity. Global Diversity Trust

Füssel, H-M. (2009). An updated assessment of the risks from climate change based on research published since the IPCC Fourth Assessment Report. *Climatic Change* published online 18 August 2009

Gao, X. and Giorgi, F. (2008). Increased aridity in the Mediterranean region under greenhouse gas forcing estimated from high resolution regional climate projections. *Global and Planetary Change* 62, 195-209

Gaunt, L.J. and Lehmann, J. (2008). Energy Balance and Emissions Associated with Biochar Sequestration and Pyrolysis Bioenergy Production. *Environmental Science & Technology* 42(11), 4152-4158

Gazeau, F., C. Quiblier, J. M. Jansen, J.-P. Gattuso, J. J. Middelburg, and Heip, C.H.R. (2007). Impact of elevated CO_2 on shellfish calcification. *Geophysical Research Letters* 34, L07603, doi:10.1029/2006GL028554.

GCOS (2009). Global Climate Observing Systems: Ensuring the Availability for Global Observations for Climate. Global Climate Observing Systems Secretariat, Geneva, Switzerland http://www.wmo.ch/pages/prog/gcos/index.php?name=Background [Accessed 14 September 2009]

Giles, K.A., Laxon, S.W. and Ridout, A.L. (2008). Circumpolar thinning of Arctic sea ice following the 2007 record ice extent minimum. *Geophysical Research Letters* 35, L22502

Gilman, S.E., Wethey, D.S. and Helmuth, B. (2006). Variation in the sensitivity of organismal body temperature to climate change over local and geographic scales. *Proceedings of the National Academy of Sciences* 103(25), 9560-9565

Gislason, S.R., Gunnlaugsson, E., Broecker, W.S., Oelkers, E.H., Matter, J.M., Stefánsson, A., Arnórsson, S., Björnsson, G, Fridriksson T and Lackner, K. (2007). Permanent CO_2 sequestration into basalt: the Hellisheidi, Iceland project. *Geophysical Research Abstracts* 9, 07153

Glaser, B. (2007). Prehistorically modified soils of central Amazonia: a model for sustainable agriculture in the twenty-first century. *Philosophical Transactions of the Royal Society* B 362, 187–196

Glazovsky, A.F. and Macheret, Yu. Ya. (2006). in *Glaciation of North and Central Eurasia at Present Time*. V. M. Kotlyakov, (Ed.) Institute of Geography of the Russian Academy of Science, Moscow

González T., Moreno, R.M., de Pisón, E.M., and Serrano, E. (2008). `Little Ice Age' glaciation and current glaciers in the Iberian Peninsula. *The Holocene* 18(4), 551

Graversen, R.G., Mauritsen, T., Tjernström, M., Källén, E. and Svensson, G. (2008). Vertical structure of recent Arctic warming. *Nature* 451, 53-56

Gregg, J.S., Andres, R.J. and Marland, G. (2008). China: Emissions pattern of the world leader in CO_2 emissions from fossil fuel consumption and cement production. *Geophysical Research Letters* 35, L08806

Griggs, D. (2001). *Climate Change 2001, Synthesis Report. Contribution of Working Groups I, II and III to the Third Assessment Report (TAR) of the Intergovernmental Panel on Climate Change (IPCC)*. Cambridge University Press, 2001

GTOS (2009). Global Terrestrial Observing System: Background Resources. GTOS http://www.fao.org/gtos/res.html [Accessed 14 September 2009]

Guinotte, J.M., Fabry, V.J. and Ann, N.Y. (2008). Ocean Acidification and Its Potential Effects on Marine Ecosystems. *Proceedings of the National Academy of Sciences* 1134, 320-342

Gullison R.E., Frumhoff, P.C., Canadell, J.G., Field, C.B., Nepstad, D.C., Hayhoe, K., Avissar, R., Curran, L.M., Friedlingstein, P., Jones, C.D. and Nobre, C. (2007). Tropical Forests and Climate Policy. *Science* 316(5827), 985-986

Haas, C., Pfaffling, A., Hendricks, S., Rabenstein, L., Etienne, J.L. and Rigor, I. (2008). Reduced ice thickness in Arctic Transpolar Drift favors rapid ice retreat. *Geophysical Research Letters* 35, L17501

Hackstock, R. (2008). Renewable Energy – The Way Forward for the Next Century. Austrian Energy Agency, Vienna. www.energyagency.at/(en)/projekte/res_overview.htm

Haeberli, W., Hoelzle, M., Paul, F. and Zemp, M. (2007). Integrated monitoring of mountain glaciers as key indicators of global climate change: the European Alps. *Annals of Glaciology* 46, 150-160

Halford, N. (2009). Crop Science for a Changing Climate and Plant Biomass for Food and Energy, Preface to Special Issue. *Journal of Experimental Botany* 60(10), 2773

Hall-Spencer, J.M., Rodolfo-Metalpa, R., Martin, S., Ransome, E., Fine, M., Turner, S.M., Rowley, S.J., Tedesco, D. and Buia, M.C. (2008). Volcanic carbon dioxide vents show ecosystem effects of ocean acidification. *Nature* 454, 96-99

Halpern, B.S, Walbridge, S., Selkoe, K.A., Kappel, C.V., Micheli, F., D'Agrosa, C., Bruno, J.F., Casey, K.S., Ebert, C., Fox, H.E., Fujtia, R., Heinemann, D., Lenihan, H.S., Madin, E.M.P., Perry, M.T., Selig, E.R., Spaling, M., Steneck, R. and Watson, R. (2008). A Global Map of Human Impact on Marine Ecosystems. *Science* 319, 948-952

Hansen, J., Sato, M., Ruedy, R., Lo, K., Lea, D.W., and Medina-Elizade, M. (2006) Global temperature change. *Proceedings of the National Academy of Sciences*, 103, 14288-14293

Hastenrath, S. (2009). Climatic forcing of glacier thinning on the mountains of equatorial East Africa. *International Journal of Climatology* 9 February 2009 10.1002/joc.1866

Hazell, P. and Wood, S. (2008). Drivers of change in global agriculture. *Philosophical Transactions of the Royal Society* 363, 495-515

Heberger, M., Cooley, H., Herrera, P., Gleick, P.H. and Moore, E. (2009). The Impacts of Sea-level Rise on the California Coast. White paper prepared for California Governor's office. Pacific Institute

Hegerl, G.C. and Solomon, S. (2009). Risks of Climate Engineering. *Science* 325, 955-956

Hegland, S.J., Nielsen, A., Lázaro, A., Bjerknes, A. and Totland, Ø. (2008). How does climate warm it affect plant-polinator interactions? *Ecology Letters* 12(2), 184-195

Hill, J., Polasky, S., Nelson, E., Tilman, D., Huo, H., Ludwig, L., Neumann, J., Zheng, H. and Bonta, D. (2009). Climate change and health costs of air emissions from biofuels and gasoline. *Proceedings of the National Academy of Sciences* 106(6), 2077-2082

Hock, R., Woul, M., Radic, V. and Dyurgerov, M. (2009). Mountain glaciers and ice caps around Antarctica make a large sea-level rise contribution. *Geophysical Research Letters* 36, 07501

Hoegh-Guldberg, O., Mumby, P.J., Hooten, A.J., Steneck, R.S., Greenfield, P., Gomez, E., Harvell, C.D., Sale, P.F., Edwards, A.J., Caldeira, K., Knowlton, N., Eakin, C.M., Iglesias-Prieto, R., Muthiga, N., Bradbury, R.H., Dubi, A. and Hatziolos, M.E. (2007). Coral Reefs Under Rapid Climate Change and Ocean Acidification. *Science* 318(5857), 1737-1742

Hoegh-Guldberg, O., Hughes, L., McIntyre, S., Lindenmayer, D.B., Parmesan, C., Possingham, H.P., Thomas, C.D. (2008). Assisted Colonization and Rapid Climate Change. *Science* 32, 345-346

Hoegh-Guldberg, O., Hoegh-Guldberg, H., Veron, J.E.N., Green, A., Gomez, E.D., Lough, J., King, M., Ambariyanto, Hansen, L., Cinner, J., Dews, G., Russ, G., Schuttenberg, H. Z., Peñaflor, E.L., Eakin, C.M., Christensen, T.R.L., Abbey, M., Areki, F., Kosaka, R.A., Tewfik, A. and Oliver, J. (2009). *The Coral Triangle and Climate Change: Ecosystems, People and Societies at Risk.* WWF Australia, Brisbane

Holden, S., Otsuka, K. and Place, F. (2008). *The Emergence of Land Markets in Africa: Impacts on Poverty, Equity, and Efficiency.* Resources for the Future Press, Washington, D.C.

Holfort J., E. Hansen, S. Østerhus, S. Dye, S. Jónsson, J. Meincke, J. Mortensen and M. Meredith (2009). Freshwater fluxes east of Greenland. In: *Arctic-Subarctic Ocean Fluxes Defining the Role of the Northern Seas in Climate.* Dickson, R.R., Meincke, J., Rhines, P. (Eds.) 2008, 304

Holland, D.M., Thomas, R.H., Young, B., Ribergaard, M.H. and Lyberth, B. (2008). Acceleration of Jakobshavn Isbræ triggered by warm subsurface ocean waters. *Nature Geoscience* 1(10), 659-664

Holman, J. D., Burnett, K. G. and Burnett, L. E. (2004). Effects of hypercapnic hypoxia on the clearance of Vibrio campbelli in the Atlantic blue crab, *Callinectes sapidus rathbun. Biological Bulletin* 206, 188–96

Hopkinson, C.S., Lugo, A.E., Alber, M., Covich, A.P. and Van Bloem, S.J. (2008). Forecasting effects of sea-level rise and windstorms on coastal and inland ecosystems. *Frontiers in Ecology and the Environment* 6(5), 255-263

Horton, R., Herweijer, C., Rosenzweig, C., Liu, J., Gornitz, V. and Ruane, A.C. (2008). Sea level rise projections for current generation CGCMs based on the semi-empirical method. *Geophysical Research Letters* 35, L02715

Howat, I.M., Joughin, I., Tulaczyk, S. and Gogineni, S. (2005). Rapid retreat and acceleration of Helheim Glacier, east Greenland, *Geophysical Research Letters* 32, L22502, doi:10.1029/2005GL024737.

Howat, I.M., Smith, B.E., Joughin, I. and Scambos, T.A. (2008). Rates of Southeast Greenland Ice Volume Loss from Combined ICESat and ASTER Observations. *Geophysical Research Letters* 35, L17505

Howden, S.M., Soussana, J-F., Tubiello, F.N., Chhetri, N., Dunlop, M. and Meinke, H. (2007). Adapting agriculture to climate change. *Proceedings of the National Academy of Sciences* 104, 19691-19696

Howell, S.E.L., Duguay, C.R. and Markus, T. (2009). Sea ice conditions and melt season duration variability within the Canadian Arctic Archipelago: 1979-2008. *Geophysical Research Letters* 36, L10502

Howes, S. (2009). Cheap but not easy: the reduction of greenhouse gas emissions from deforestation and forest degradation in Papua New Guinea. *Pacific Economic Bulletin* 24(1), 130-143

Hunter, J.R. (2009). Estimating sea-level extremes under conditions of uncertain sea-level rise. *Climatic Change*, DOI 10.1007/s10584-009-9671-6

Huss, A. and Fahrländer, B. (2007). *Tick-borne diseases in Switzerland and climate change.* Institute of Social and Preventive Medicine, University of Basel

IAASTD (2008). Executive Summary of the Synthesis Report. International Assessment of Agricultural Knowledge, Science and Technology for Development

ICIMOD (2007). Bajracharya, Samjwal R., Pradeep K. Mool, and Basanta R. Shrestha. Impact of Climate Change on Himalayan Glaciers and Glacial Lakes. Case Studies on GLOF and Associated Hazards in Nepal and Bhutan. ICIMOD, Kathmandu, Nepal: Quality Printers (Pvt) Ltd.

ICIMOD (2009). Eriksson, M., Juanchu, X., Shrestha, A.B., Vaidva, R., Nepal, S., Sandstorm, K. The Changing Himalayas: Impact of Climate Change on Water Resources and Livelihoods in the Greater Himalayas.

IEA (2008a). *World Energy Outlook 2008*, OECD/International Energy Agency, Paris http://www.worldenergyoutlook.org/2007.asp

IEA (2008b). *Energy Technology Perspectives 2008*: Scenarios and Strategies to 2050, OECD/International Energy Agency, Paris

Iglesias, A., Garrote, L., Flores, F. and Moneo, M. (2007). Challenges to Manage the Risk of Water Scarcity and Climate Change in the Mediterranean. *Water Resources Management* 21(5), 775-788

Ilyina, T., Zeebe, R.E., Maier-Reimer, E. and Heinze, C. (2009). Early detection of ocean acidification effects on marine calcification. *Global Biogeochemical Cycles* 23, GB1008

IMO (2007). Large-scale ocean fertilization operations not currently justified. Press briefing, International Maritime Organization. www.imo.org [Accessed 20 August 2009]

IPCC (2007a). *Climate Change 2007: The physical science basis.* Contribution of Working Group I to the Fourth Assessment Report of the Intergovernmental Panel on Climate Change, Cambridge University Press, New York

IPCC (2007b). *Climate Change 2007: Impacts, Adaptation and Vulnerability.* Contribution of Working Group II to the Fourth Assessment Report of the Intergovernmental Panel on Climate Change, Cambridge University Press, New York

IPCC (2007c). *Climate Change 2007: Mitigation of Climate Change.* Contribution of Working Group III to the Fourth Assessment Report of the Intergovernmental Panel on Climate Change, Cambridge University Press, New York

IPY (2009). International Polar Year 2007-2009. www.antarctica.ac.uk/indepth/ipy/index.php

Ise, T., Dunn, A.L., Wofsy, S.C. and Moorcroft, P.R. (2008). High sensitivity of peat decomposition to climate change through water-table feedback. *Nature Geoscience* 1, 763-766

IUFRO (2009). Making forests fit for climate change: A global view of climate-change impacts on forests and people and options for adaptation. International Union of Forest Research Organizations

Jackson, J.B.C. (2008). Ecological extinction and evolution in the brave new ocean. *Proceedings of the National Academy of Sciences* 105, 11458-11465

Jackson, R. (2009). Geoengineering To Mitigate Global Warming May Cause Other Environmental Harm. *Science Daily*, August 7, 2009

Jackson, R.B., Randerson, J.T., Canadell, J.G., Anderson, R.G., Avissar, R., Baldocchi, D.D., Bonan, G.B., Caldeira, K., Diffenbaugh, N.S., Field, C.B., Hungate, B.A., Jobbagy, E.G., Kueppers, L.M., Nosetto, M.D. and Pataki, D.E. (2008). Protecting climate with forests. *Environmental Research Letters* 3, 044006

Jevrejeva, S., Moore, J.C., Grinsted, A. and Woodworth, P.L. (2008). Recent global sea level acceleration started over 200 years ago? *Geophysical Research Letters* 35, L08715

Johannessen, O.M. (2008). Decreasing Arctic Sea Ice Mirrors Increasing CO_2 on Decadal Time Scale. *Atmospheric And Oceanic Science Letters* 1(1), 51-56

Johanson, C.M. and Fu, Q. (2009). Hadley Cell Widening: Model Simulations versus Observations. *Journal of Climate* 22, 2713-2725

Jones, C., Lowe, J., Spencer, L. and Betts, R. (2009). Committed terrestrial ecosystem changes due to climate change. *Nature Geoscience* 2, 484-486

Jones, P.D., Parker, D.E., Osborn, T.J. and Briffa, K.R. (2008). Global and hemispheric temperature anomalies – Land and marine instrumental records. In *Trends: A Compendium of Data on Global Change.* Carbon Dioxide Information Analysis Center, Oak Ridge National Laboratory, U.S. Department of Energy

Joughin, I., Das, S.B., King, M.A., Smith, B.E., Howat, I.M. and Moon, T. (2008). Seasonal speedup along the western flank of the Greenland ice sheet. *Science* 320, 781-783

Kairo, J.G., Lang'at, J.K.S., Dahdouh, F., Bosire, J. and Karachi, M. (2008). Structural development and productivity of replanted mangrove plantations in Kenya. *Forest Ecology and Management* 255(7), 2670-2677

Karl, T.R, Melillo, J.M., and Peterson, T.C. (2009). Global Climate Change Impacts in the United States. Cambridge University Press

Karsenty, A., Guéneau, S., Capistrano, D., Singer, B. and Peyron, J.L. (2008). Summary of the Proceedings of the International Workshop "The International Regime, Avoided Deforestation and the Evolution of Public and Private Policies Towards Forests in Developing Countries" held in Paris, 21-23 November 2007. *International Forestry Review* 10(3), 424-428

Kay, J.E., L'Ecuyer, T., Gettelman, A., Stephens, G. and O'Dell, C. (2008). The contribution of cloud and radiation anomalies to the 2007 Arctic sea ice extent minimum. *Geophysical Research Letters* 35, L08503

Keeling, C.D. and Whorf, T.P. (2005). Atmospheric CO_2 records from sites in the SIO air sampling network. In *Trends: A Compendium of Data on Global Change.* Carbon Dioxide Information Analysis Center, Oak Ridge National Laboratory, U.S. Department of Energy, Oak Ridge, Tenn., U.S.A.

Keeling R.F., Piper, S.C., Bollenbacher, A.F. and Walker, J.S. (2009). Atmospheric CO_2 records from sites in the SIO air sampling network. In *Trends: A Compendium of Data on Global Change.* Carbon Dioxide Information Analysis Center, Oak Ridge National Laboratory, U.S. Department of Energy, Oak Ridge, Tenn., U.S.A.

Kehrwald, N.M., Thompson, L.G., Tandong, Y., Mosley-Thompson, E., Schotterer, U., Alfimov, V., Beer, J., Eikenberg, J. and Davis, M.E. (2008). Mass loss on Himalayan glacier endangers water resources. *Geophysical Research Letters* 35, L22503

Kelly, A.E. and Goulden, M.L. (2008). Rapid shifts in plant distribution with recent climate change. *Proceedings of the National Academy of Sciences* 105(33), 11823-11826

Killeen, T.J., Douglas, M., Consiglio, T., Jørgensen, P.M. and Mejia, J. (2007). Wet spots and dry spots in the Andean hotspot. *Journal of Biogeography* 34, 1357-1373

Klein, R.J.T., Alam, M., Burton, I., Dougherty, W.W., Ebi, K.L., Fernandes, M., Huber-Lee, A., Rahman, A.A. and Swartz, C. (2006). Application of Environmentally Sound Technologies for Adaptation to Climate Change. Technical Paper FCCC/TP/2006/2, United Nations Framework Convention on Climate Change Secretariat, Bonn, Germany, 107 pp

Kleiner, K. (2009). *The bright prospect of biochar.* Nature Reports Climate Change. http://www.nature.com/climate/2009/0906/full/climate.2009.48.html

Kleypas, J. A., Feely, R. A., Fabry, V. J., Langdon, C., Sabine, C. L. Robbins, L. L. (2006). Impacts of Ocean Acidification on Coral Reefs and Other Marine Calcifiers. A Guide for Future Research. Report of a workshop sponsored by NSF, NOAA & USGS.

Klotzbach, P.J. (2006). Trends in global tropical cyclone activity over the past twenty years (1986-2005). *Geophysical Research Letters* 33, L010805

Knapp, A.K., Beier, C., Briske,D.D., Classen, A.T., Luo, Y., Reichstein, M., Smith, M.D., Smith, S.D., Bell, J.E., Fay, P.A., Heisler, J.L., Leavitt, S.W., Sherry, R., Smith, B. and Weng., E. (2008). Consequences of More Extreme Precipitation Regimes for Terrestrial Ecosystems. *BioScience* 58(9), 811-821

Kröpelin, S., Verschuren, D., Lézine, A-M., Eggermont, H., Cocquyt, C., Francus, P., Cazet, J-P., Fagot, M., Rumes, B., Russell, J.M., Darius, F., Conley, D.J., Schuster, M., Suchodoletz, H. and Engstrom, D.R. (2008). Climate-Driven Ecosystem Succession in the Sahara: The Past 6000 Years. *Science* 320(5877), 765-768

Kurihara, H., Kato, S. and Ishimatsu, A. (2007). Effects of increased seawater pCO_2 on early development of the oyster *Crassostrea gigas. Aquatic Biology* 1, 91–8

Kurihara, H., Asai, T., Kato, S. and Ishimatsu, A. (2009). Effects of elevated pCO_2 on early development in the mussel *Mytilus galloprovincialis. Aquatic Biology* 4, 225–33

Kurz, W.A., Dymond, C.C., Stinson, G., Rampley, G.J., Neilson, E.T., Carroll, A.L., Ebata, T. and Safranyik, L. (2008). Mountain pine beetle and forest carbon feedback to climate change. *Nature* 452, 987-990

Kwok, R., Cunningham, G.F., Wensnahan, M., Rigor, I., Zwally, H.J. and Yi, D. (2009). Thinning and volume loss of the Arctic Ocean sea ice cover: 2003-2008. *Journal of Geophysical Research* 114, C07005

Kwon, E.Y., Primeau, F. and Sarmiento, J.L. (2009). The impact of remineralization depth on the air-sea carbon balance. *Nature Geoscience* 2, 630-635

Lackner, K. and Liu, P. (2008). Removal of Carbon Dioxide from Air. The International Bureau, The World Intellectual Property Organization

Larsen, C.F., Motyka, R.J., Arendt, A.A., Echelmeyer, K.A. and Geissler, P.E. (2007). Glacier changes in southeast Alaska and northwest British Columbia and contribution to sea level rise. *Journal of Geophysical Research Letters* 112, F01007

Lawler, J.J., Shafer, S.L., White, D., Kareiva, P., Maurer, E.P., Blaustein, A.R. and Bartlein, P.J. (2009). Projected climate-induced faunal change in the Western Hemisphere. *Ecology* 90(3), 588-597

Lawrence, D.M., Slater, A.G., Tomas, R.A., Holland, M.M. and Deser, C. (2009). Accelerated Arctic land warming and permafrost degradation during rapid sea ice loss. *Geophysical Research Letters* 35, 11506

Lehmann, J. (2007). A handful of carbon. *Nature* 447, 143-144

Lenoir, J., Gegout, J.C., Marquet, P.A., de Ruffray, P. and Brisse, H. (2008). A Significant Upward Shift in Plant Species Optimum Elevation During the 20th Century. *Science* 320(5884), 1768-1771

Lenton, A., Codron, F., Bopp, L., Metzl, N., Cadule, P., Tagliabue, A. and Le Sommer, J. (2009). Stratospheric ozone depletion reduces ocean carbon uptake and enhances ocean acidification. *Geophysical Research Letters* 36, L12606

Lenton, T.M. and Vaughan, N.E. (2009). Radiative forcing potential of climate geoengineering. *Atmospheric Chemistry and Physics Discussions* 9, 1-50

Lenton, T.M., Held, H., Kriegler, E., Hall, J.W., Lucht, W., Rahmstorf, S. and Schellnhuber, H.J. (2008). Tipping elements in the Earth's climate system. *Proceedings of the National Academy of Sciences* 105(6), 1786-1793

Le Quéré, C., Rödenbeck, C., Buitenhuis, E.T., Conway, T.J., Langenfelds, R., Gomez, A., Labuschagne, C., Ramonet, M., Nakazawa, T., Metzl, N., Gillett, N. and Heimann, M. (2007). Saturation of the Southern Ocean CO_2 Sink Due to Recent Climate Change. *Science* 316(5832), 1735-1738

Lettenmaier, D.P. and Milly, P.C.D. (2009). Land waters and sea level. *Nature Geoscience* 2, 452-454

Li, B., Nychka, D.W. and Ammann, C. (2007). The 'hockey stick' and the 1990s: a statistical perspective on reconstructing hemispheric temperatures. *Tellus* 59A, 591–598

Lionello, P., Plantod, S. and Rodod, X. (2008). Trends and climate change in the Mediterranean region. *Global and Planetary Change* 63(2-3), 87-89

Liu, G. and Han, S. (2009). Long-term forest management and timely transfer of carbon into wood products help reduce atmospheric carbon. *Ecological Modelling* 220, 1719-1723

Lovelock, J.E. and Rapley, C.G. (2007). Ocean pipes could help the earth to cure itself. *Nature* 449, 403

Lozier, S. (2009). Overturning assumptions. *Nature Geoscience* 2, 12-13

Lu, J., Deser, C. and Reichler, T. (2009). Cause of the widening of the tropical belt since 1958. *Geophysical Research Letters* 36, L02803

Lumsden, S.E., Hourigan, T.F., Bruckner A.W. and Dorr, G. (eds.) (2007). The State of Deep Coral Ecosystems of the United States. NOAA Technical Memorandum CRCP-3, Silver Spring, Maryland

Lunt, D.J., Ridgwell, A., Valdes, P.J. and Seale, A. (2008). "Sunshade World": A fully coupled GCM evaluation of the climatic impacts of geoengineering. *Geophysical Research Letters* 35, L12710

Lyon, B.E., Chaine, A.S., and Winkler, D.W. (2008). A Matter of Timing. *Science* 321(5892), 1051-1052

MA (2005). Millennium Ecosystem Assessment. *Ecosystems and Human Well-being: Policy Responses, Volume 3.* Chopra, K., Leemans, R., Kumar, P., Simons, H. (eds.) Washington D.C., USA, Island Press

MacDonald, G.M., Bennett, K.D., Jackson, S.T., Parducci, L., Smith, F.A., Smol, J.P. and Willis, K.J. (2008). Impacts of climate change on species, populations and communities: palaeobiogeographical insights and frontiers. *Progress in Physical Geography* 32(2), 139-172

MacLeod, E. and Salm. R.V. (2006). Managing Mangroves for Resilience to Climate Change. IUCN, Gland, Switzerland

MacLeod, E., Salm, R., Green, A. and Almany, J. (2008). Designing marine protected area networks to address the impacts of climate change. *Frontiers in Ecology and the Environment e-View*

Mair, D., Burgess, D., Sharp, M., Dowdeswell, J.A., Benham, T., Marshall, S. and Cawkwell, F. (2009). Mass balance of the Prince of Wales Icefield, Ellesmere Island, Nunavut, Canada. *Journal of Geophysical Research*, 114

Malhi, Y., Roberts, J.T., Betts, R.A., Killeen, T.J., Li, W. and Nobre, C.A. (2008). Climate change, deforestation, and the fate of the Amazon. *Science* 319(5860), 169-172

Manabe, S. and Stouffer, R.J. (1995). Simulation of abrupt climate change induced by freshwater input to the North Atlantic Ocean. *Nature* 378, 165-167

Mars, J.C. and Houseknecht, D.W. (2007). Quantitative remote sensing study indicates doubling of coastal erosion rate in past 50 yr along a segment of the Arctic coast of Alaska. *Geology* 35(7), 583-586

Masiokas, M.H., Villalba, R., Luckman, B.H., Lascano, M.E., Delgado, S. and Stepanek, P. (2008). 20th-Century Glacier recession and regional hydroclimatic changes in northwestern Patagonia. *Global and Planetary Change* 60(1-2), 85-100

Maslanik, J., Fowler, A.C., Stroeve, J., Drobot, S., Zwally, J., Yi, D. and Emery, W. (2007). A younger, thinner Arctic ice cover: Increased potential for rapid, extensive sea-ice loss. *Geophysical Research Letters* 34, L24501

Matthews, H.D. and Caldeira, K. (2007). Transient climate-carbon simulations of planetary geoengineering. *Proceedings of the National Academy of Sciences* 104, 9949–9954

Mayewski, P.A., Meredith, M.P., Summerhayes, C.P., Turner, J., Worby, A., Barrett, P.J., Casassa, G., Bertler, N.A.N., Bracegirdle, T., Naveira Garabato, A.C., Bromwich, D.H., Campbell, H., Hamilton, G.S., Lyons, W.B., Maasch, K.A., Aoki, S., Xiao, C. and Ommen, T. (2009). State of the Antarctic and Southern Ocean climate system. *Reviews of Geophysics* 47, RG1003

McCarthy, J.J., Canziani, O.F., Leary, N.A., Dokken, D.J., White, K.S. (2001). *Climate Change 2001: Impacts, Adaptation, and Vulnerability.* Contribution of Working Group II to the Third Assessment Report of the Intergovernmental Panel on Climate Change, Cambridge University Press, United Kingdom

McHenry, M.P. (2009). Agricultural bio-char production, renewable energy generation and farm carbon sequestration in Western Australia: Certainty, uncertainty and risk. *Agriculture, Ecosystems and Environment* 129, 1-7

McLachlan, J.S., Hellmann, J.J. and Schwartz M.W. (2007). A framework for debate of assisted migration in an era of climate change. *Conservation Biology* 21, 297–302

McPhee, M.G., Proshutinsky, A., Morison, J.H., Steele, M. and Alkire, M.B. (2009). Rapid change in freshwater content of the Arctic Ocean. *Geophysical Research Letters* 36, L10602

Meehl, G.A., Goddard, L., Murphy, J., Stouffer R.J., and Boer, G. (2009). Decadal Prediction: Can it be skillful? *Bulletin of the American Meteorological Society*: In Press

Meier, M.F, Dyurgerov, M.B., Rick, U.K., O'Neel, S., Pfeffer, W.T., Anderson, R.S., Anderson, S.P. and Glazovsky, A.F. (2007). Glaciers Dominate Eustatic Sea-Level Rise in the 21st Century. *Science* 317(5841), 1064-7

Meinshausen, M., Meinshausen, N., Hare, W., Raper, S.C.B., Frieler, K., Knutti, R., Frame, D.J. and Allen, M.R. (2009). Greenhouse-gas emission targets for limiting global warming to 2°C. *Nature* 458, 1158-1162

Metz, B. Davidson, O.R., Bosch, P.R., Dave, R. and Meyer, L.A. (2007). (eds). Climate Change 2007: Mitigation of Climate Change. Contribution of Working Group III to the Fourth Assessment Report of the Intergovernmental Panel on Climate Change, 2007. Cambridge University Press, Cambridge, United Kingdom and New York, NY, USA

Mignon, B.K., Socolow, R.H., Sarmiento, J.L. and Oppenheimer, M. (2008). Atmospheric stabilization and the timing of carbon mitigation. *Climatic Change* 88, 251-265

Miles, E.L. (2009). On the Increasing Vulnerability of the World Ocean to Multiple Stresses. *Annual Review of Environment and Resources* 34(18), 1-18

Milne G., Gehrels W.R., Hughes C. and Tamisiea M. (2009). Identifying the causes of sea level changes, *Nature Geoscience* 2, 471-478

Mohammed, A-J. and Whimore, A. (2009). "Realistic Costs of Carbon Capture." Discussion Paper 2009-08, Energy Technology Innovation Research Group, Belfer Center for Science and International Affairs, Harvard Kennedy School, July 2009

Monaghan, A.J., Bromwich, D.H., Chapman, W. and Comiso, J.C. (2008). Recent variability and trends of Antarctic near-surface temperature. *Journal of Geophysical Research* 113, D04105

Montgomery, R.D. (2008). Why We Need Another Agricultural Revolution. In *Dirt: The Erosion of Civilizations*. University of California Press.

Moore, F. C. and MacCracken, M.C. (2009). Lifetime-leveraging: An approach to achieving international agreement and effective climate protection using mitigation of short-lived greenhouse gases. (In Press)

Moore, R.D., Fleming, S.W., Menounos, B., Wheate, R., Fountain, A., Stahl, K., Holm, K., and Jakob, M. (2009). Glacier change in western North America: implications for hydrology, geomorphic hazards and water quality. *Hydrological Processes* 23, 42-61

Morton, J. (2007). The impact of climate change on smallholder and subsistence agriculture. *Proceedings of the National Academy of Sciences* 104, 19680-19685

Mote, T.L. (2007). Greenland surface melt trends 1973–2007: Evidence of a large increase in 2007. *Geophysical Research Letters* 34, L22507

Mottram, R., Nielsen, C., Ahlstrøm, A.P., Reeh, N., Kristensen, S.S., Christensen, E.L., Forsberg, R., and Stenseng, L. (2009). A new regional high-resolution map of basal and surface topography for the Greenland ice-sheet margin at Paakitsoq, West Greenland. *Annals of Glaciology*, 50, 105-111(7)

Mueller, D. R., L. Copland, A. Hamilton, and D. Stern (2008). Examining Arctic Ice Shelves Prior to the 2008 Breakup, *EOS, Transactions American Geophysical Union* 89(49), 1029

Murphy, B.F. and Timbal, B. (2008). A review of recent climate variability and climate change in southeastern Australia. *International Journal of Climatology* 28(7), 859-879

NASA (2005). Thermohaline circulation. Map by Robert Simmon, adapted from the IPCC 2001 and Rahmstorf 2002. National Aeronautics and Space Administration NASA http://earthobservatory.nasa.gov/

NASA (2006a). Twinned GRACE satellites. National Aeronautics and Space Administration NASA http://www.csr.utexas.edu/grace

NASA (2006b). Sunderbans Protected Area Image of the day, October 15, 2006. National Aeronautics and Space Administration NASA http://earthobservatory.nasa.gov

NASA (2007). Image by Robert Simmon, based on data from Joey Comiso, GSFC. National Aeronautics and Space Administration NASA http://earthobservatory.nasa.gov

NASA (2008). Irrawaddy River Delta. National Aeronautics and Space Administration MODIS Rapid Response Team http://earthobservatory.nasa.gov/NaturalHazards

NASA (2009). Goddard Space Flight Center Scientific Visualization Studio. Historic calving front locations courtesy of Anker Weidick and Ole Bennike, Geological Survey of Denmark and Greenland. National Aeronautics and Space Administration Data courtesy of Landsat-7/ETM+

NASA JPL (2008). Gravity Recovery and Climate Experiment (GRACE). National Aeronautics and Space Administration and Jet Propulsion Laboratory. http://podaac.jpl.nasa.gov/grace/

NASA JPL (2009). Ocean Bottom Pressure Data from GRACE Sheds Light on Ocean, Climate. http://grace.jpl.nasa.gov/

National Geographic (2007). The acid threat in November 2007. National Geographic map, November 2007

Nellemann, C., Hain, S. and Alder, J. (Eds). (2008). *In Dead Water – Merging of climate change with pollution, over-harvest, and infestations in the world's fishing grounds.* United Nations Environment Programme, GRID-Arendal, Norway

Ngongi, N. (2008). Policy Implications of High Food Prices for Africa. Alliance for a Green Revolution in Africa

Nick, F. M., Vieli, A., Howat, I.M. and Joughin, I. (2009). Large-scale changes in Greenland outlet glacier dynamics triggered at the terminus. *Nature Geoscience*, 2(2) 110-114

NOAA (2007). http://www.ncdc.noaa.gov/img/climate/research/2007/ann/significant-extremes2007.gif National Climatic Data Center

NOAA (2008). http://www.ncdc.noaa.gov/img/climate/research/2008/ann/significant-extremes2008.gif National Climatic Data Center

NOAA (2009a). http://www.ncdc.noaa.gov/climate-monitoring/ index.php National Climatic Data Center

NOAA (2009b). http://www.osdpd.noaa.gov/ml/ocean/sst/anomaly.html Current Operational SST Anomaly Chart for the Year 2009. National Oceanic and Atmospheric Administration (NOAA)

NOAA-ESRL (2008). http://www.esrl.noaa.gov/gmd/obop/spo/igy_history.html International Geophysical Year: IGY History. National Oceanic and Atmospheric Administration, Earth System Research Laboratory

Norström, A., Nyström, M., Lokrantz, J., Folke, C., (2009). Alternative states of coral reefs: beyond coral-macroalgal phase shifts. *Marine Ecology Progress Series*, Vol. 376, 295-306, 2009

NPI (2009). Norwegian Polar Institute. Polar Research. http://website.lineone.net/~polar. publishing/norwegianpolarinstitute.htm

NSIDC (2009a). *Arctic sea ice news and analysis.* National Snow and Data Centre. http://nsidc. org/arcticseaicenews

NSIDC (2009b). Antarctic Sea Ice Concentration on September 4, 2009. National Snow and Ice Data Center. http://nsidc.org/data/seaice_index/

Oerlemans, J., Giesen, R. H. and van den Broeke, M.R. (2009). Retreating alpine glaciers: increased melt rates due to accumulation of dust (Vadret da Morteratsch, Switzerland). *Journal of Glaciology* 55 (192), 729-736

Oestreicher, J.S., Benessaiah, K., Ruiz-Jaen, M.C., Sloan, S., Turner, K., Pelletier, J., Guay, B., Clark, K.E., Roche, D.G., Meiners, M. and Potvin, C. (2009). Avoiding deforestation in Panamanian protected areas: An analysis of protection effectiveness and implications for reducing emissions from deforestation and forest degradation. *Global Environmental Change* 19, 279-291

Oldenborgh, G.J., Drijfhout, S., Ulden, A., Haarsma, R., Sterl, A., Severijns, C., Hazeleger, W. and Dijkstra, H. (2008). Western Europe is warming much faster than expected. *Climate of the Past* 4, 897-928

Oliver, T.A. and Palumbi, S.R. (2009). Distributions of stress-resistant coral symbionts match environmental patterns at local but not regional scales. *Marine Ecology Progress Series* 378, 93-103

Orr, J.C., Fabry, V.J., Aumont, O., Bopp, L., Doney, S.C., Feely, R.A., Gnanadesikan, A., Gruber, N., Ishida, A., Joos, F., Key, R.M., Lindsay, K., Maier-Reimer, E., Matear, R., Monfray, P., Mouchet, A., Najjar, R.G., Plattner, G.K., Rodgers, K.B., Sabine, C.L., Sarmiento, J.L., Schlitzer, R., Slater, R.D., Totterdell, I.J., Weirig, M.F., Yamanaka, Y. and Yool, A. (2005). Anthropogenic ocean acidification over the twenty-first century and its impact on calcifying organisms. *Nature* 437(7059), 681-686

Overland, J.E. (2009). Meteorology of the Beaufort Sea. *Journal of Geophysical Research* 114, C00A07

Parizek, B.R. and R.B. Alley (2005). Implications of increased Greenland surface melt under global-warming scenarios: ice-sheet simulations. *Quarternary Science Reviews* 23, pp. 1013-1227

Parkins, J.R. and McKendrick, N.A. (2007). Assessing community vulnerability: a study of the mountain pine beetle outbreak in British Columbia, Canada. *Global Environmental Change* 17, 460-471

Parmesan, C. (2006). Ecological and evolutionary responses to recent climate change. *Annual Review of Ecology, Evolution, and Systematics* 37, 637-669

Parry, M.L., Canziani, O.F., Palutikof, J.P. , van der Linden, P.J. and Hanson, C.E. (2007). Eds.: IPCC, Climate Change 2007: Impacts, Adaptation and Vulnerability. Contribution of Working Group II to the Fourth Assessment Report of the Intergovernmental Panel on Climate Change, Cambridge University Press, Cambridge, UK

Pauchard, A., Kueffer, C., Dietz, H, Daehler, C.C., Alexander, J., Edwards, P.J., Arévalo, J.R., Cavieres, L.A., Guisan, A., Haider, S., Jakobs, G., McDougall, K., Millar, C.I., Naylor, B.J., Parks, C.G., Rew. L.J. and Seipel, T. (2009). Ain't no mountain high enough: plant invasions reaching new elevations. *Frontiers in Ecology and the Environment* 7

Paytan, A., Mackey, K.R.M., Chen, Y., Lima, I.D., Doney, S.C., Mahowald, N., Labiosa, R. and Post, A.F. (2009). Toxicity of atmospheric aerosols on marine phytoplankton. *Proceedings of the National Academy of Sciences* 106(12), 4601-4605

Peltier R. (2009). Closure of the budget of global sea level rise over the GRACE era: the importance and magnitudes of the required corrections for global glacial isostatic adjustment. *Quarternary Science Reviews* 28(17-18), 1658-1674

Pfeffer, W.T. (2007). A Simple Mechanism for Irreversible Tidewater Glacier Retreat. *Journal of Geophysical Research* (Earth Surface) 112, F3

Pfeffer, W.T., Harper, J.T. and O'Neel, S. (2008). Kinematic Constraints on Glacier Contributions to 21st-Century Sea-Level Rise. *Science* 321(5894): 1340-1343

Pfeffer, W.T. (2009). Personal communication, August 2009

Phillips, O.L., Lewis, S.L., Baker, T.R., Chao, K-J. and Higuchi, N. (2008). The changing Amazon forest. *Philosophical Transactions of the Royal Society* B 363, 1819-1827

Phillips, O.L., Aragão, L.E.O.C, Lewis, S.L., Fisher, J.B., Lloyd, J., López-González, G., Malhi, Y., Monteagudo, A., Peacock, J., Quesada, C.A., Heijden, G., Almeida, S., Amaral, I., Arroyo, L., Aymard, G., Baker, T.R., Bánki, O., Blanc, L., Bonal, D., Brando, P., Chave, J., Oliveira, A.C.A., Cardozo, N.D., Czimczik, C.I., Feldpausch, T.R., Freitas, M.A., Gloor, E., Higuchi, N., Jiménez, E., Lloyd, G., Meir, P., Mendoza, C., Morel, A., Neill, D.A., Nepstad, D., Patiño, S., Peñuela, M.C., Prieto, A., Ramírez, F., Schwarz, M., Silva, J., Silveira, M., Thomas, A.S., Steege, H., Stropp, J., Vásquez, R., Zelazowski, P., Dávila, E.A., Andelman, S., Andrade, A., Chao, K., Erwin, T., Fiore, A., Honorio, E.C., Keeling, H., Killeen, T.J., Laurance, W.F., Cruz, A.P., Pitman, N.C.A., Vargas, N., Ramírez-Angulo, H., Rudas, A., Salamão, R., Silva, N., Terborgh, J. and Torres-Lezama, A. (2009). Drought Sensitivity of the Amazon Rainforest. *Science* 323(5919), 1344-1347

Plattner, G. (2009). Climate change: Terrestrial ecosystem inertia. *Nature Geoscience* 2(7), 467-468

Pörtner, H.O., and Farrell, A.P. (2008). Ecology: Physiology and Climate Change. *Science* 322(5902), 690-692

Post, E., Pedersen,C., Wilmers, C. and Forchhammer, M.C. (2008). Warming, plant phenology and the spatial dimension of trophic mismatch for large herbivores. *Proceedings of the Royal Society* B 275, 2005-2013

Preskett, L., Huberman, D., Bowen-Jones, E., Edwards, G. and Brown, J. (2008). Making REDD Work for the Poor. Draft final report prepared for the Poverty Environment Partnership

Pretty, J. (2008). Agricultural Sustainability: Concepts, Principles and Evidence. *Philosophical Transactions of the Royal Society* B 363(1491), 447-465

Proshutinsky, A.Y., Morison, J., Ashik, I., Carmack, E., Frolov, I.E., Gascard, J.C., Itoh, M., Krishfield, R., McLauchlin, F., Polyakov, I.V., Rudels, B, Schauer, U., Shimada, K., Sokolov, V.T., Steele, M., Timmermans, M.-L., Toole, D.A. (2008). The Poles: Ocean, In State of the Climate in 2007, Special Supplement to BAMS 89(7), S86-S89

Proshutinsky, A., Krishfield, R., Timmermans, M-L., Toole, J., Carmack, E., McLaughlin, F., Williams, W.J., Zimmermann, S., Itoh, M. and Shimada, K. (2009). Beaufort Gyre freshwater reservoir: State and variability from observations. *Journal of Geophysical Research* 114, C00A10

Puig, P., Palanques, A., Orange, D.L., Lastras, G., and Canals, M. (2008). Dense shelf water cascades and sedimentary furrow formation in the Cap de Creus Canyon, northwestern Mediterranean Sea. *Continental Shelf Research* 1381

Rahel, F.J., and Olden, J.D. (2008). Assessing the effects of climate change on Aquatic invasive species. *Conservation Biology* 32, 203-209

Rahmstorf, S., Cazenave, A., Church, J.A., Hansen, J.E., Keeling, R.F., Parker, D.E. and Somerville, R.C.J. (2009). Recent Climate Observations Compared to Projections. *Science* 316(5825), 709

Ramanathan, V. and Carmichael, G. (2008). Global and regional climate changes due to black carbon. *Nature Geoscience* 1, 221-227

Ramanathan, V. and Feng, Y. (2008). On avoiding dangerous anthropogenic interference with the climate system: Formidable challenges ahead. *Proceedings of the National Academy of Sciences* 105(38), 14245-14250

Rasch, P.J., Tilmes, S., Turco, R.P., Robock, A., Oman, L., Chen, C-C., Stenchikov, G.L. and Garcia, R.R. (2008). An overview of Geoengineering of Climate using Stratospheric Sulfate Aerosols. *Philosophical Transactions of the Royal Society* A 366(1882), 4007-4037

Raupach, M.R., Marland, G., Ciais, P., Le Quéré, C., Canadell, J.G., Klepper, G. and Field, C.B. (2007). Global and regional drivers of accelerating CO_2 emissions. *Proceedings of the National Academy of Sciences* 104(24), 10288-10293

Rhemtulla, J.M., Mladenoff, D.J. and Clayton, M.K. (2009). Historical forest baselines reveal potential for continued carbon sequestration. *Proceedings of the National Academy of Sciences* 106, 6082-6087

Richardson, K., Steffen, W., Schellnhuber, H.J., Alcamo, J., Barker, T., Kammen, D.M., Leemans, R., Liverman, D., Munasinghe, M., Osman-Elasha, B. Stern, N. and Wæver, O. (2009). Synthesis Report: Climate Change, Global Risks, Challenges and Decisions. University of Copenhagen, Denmark

Richter, D., McCreery, L.R., Nemestothy, K.P., Jenkins, D.H., Karakash J.T., Knight J. (2009). Wood Energy in America. *Science* 323, 1432-1433

Ries, J.B., Cohen, A.L., and McCorkle, D. (2008a). Marine biocalcifiers exhibit mixed responses to CO_2-induced ocean acidification, in: *11th International Coral Reef Symposium*, Fort Lauderdale, Florida, USA, 7–11 July 2008, 229, 2008

Ries, J.B., Cohen, A.L. and McCorkle, D. C. (2008b). The mineralogical responses of marine calcifiers to CO_2-induced ocean acidification. *EOS, Transactions, American Geophysical Union* 89, OS33E-04

Rignot, E., Box, J.E., Burgess, E. and Hanna, E. (2008). Mass balance of the Greenland ice sheet from 1958 to 2007. *Geophysical Research Letters* 35, L20502

Robock, A. (2008a). 20 reasons why geoengineering may be a bad idea. *Bulletin of the Atomic Scientists* 64(2), 14-18

Robock, A. (2008b). Whither Geoengineering? *Science* 320, 1166-1167

Rodell, M., Velicogna, I. and Famiglietti, J.S. (2009). Satellite-based estimates of groundwater depletion in India. *Nature* 460, 999-1002

Rohling, E.J., Grant, K., Bolshaw, M., Roberts, A.P., Siddall, M., Hemleben, C. and Kucera, M. (2009). Antarctic temperature and global sea level closely coupled over the past five glacial cycles. *Nature Geoscience*, 2, 500-504

Rosenzweig, C., Karoly, D., Vicarelli, M., Neofotis, P., Wu, Q., Casassa, G., Menzel, A., Root, T.L., Estrella, N., Seguin, B., Tryjanowski, P., Liu, C., Rawlins, S. and Imeson, A. (2008). Attributing physical and biological impacts to anthropogenic climate change. *Nature* 453(7193), 296-297

Ross, M.S., O'Brien, J.J., Ford, R.G., Zhang, K. and Morkill, A. (2008). Disturbance and the rising tide: the challenge of biodiversity management on low-island ecosystems. *Frontiers in Ecology and the Environment e-View*

Royal Society (2009). Geoengineering the climate: science, governance and uncertainty. The Royal Society

Ruesch, A.S. and Gibbs, H. (2008). New Global Biomass Carbon Map for the Year 2000 Based on IPCC Tier-1 Methodology. Oak Ridge National Laboratory's Carbon Dioxide Information Analysis Center: Oak Ridge, USA. Available online from the Carbon Dioxide Information Analysis Center

Running, S.W. and Mills, L.S. (2009). Terrestrial Ecosystem Adaptation. Resources for the Future report

Sabine, C.L., Feely, R.A., Gruber, N., Key, R.M., Lee, K., Bullister, J.L., Wanninkhof, R., Wong, C.S., Wallace, D.W.R., Tilbrook, B., Millero, F.J., Peng, T-H., Kozyr, A., Ono, T. and Rios, A.F. (2004). The Oceanic Sink for Anthropogenic CO_2. Science 305, 367

Sachs, J.P., Sachse, D., Smittenberg, R.H., Zhang, Z., Battisti, D.S. and Golubic, S. (2009). Southward movement of the Pacific intertropical convergence zone AD 1400-1850. Nature Geoscience 2, 519-525

Sanghi, A. and Mendelsohn, R. (2008). The impacts of global warming on farmers in Brazil and India. Global Environmental Change 18, 655-665

Scheffer, M., Carpenter, S., Foley, J.A., Folke, C. and Walker, B. (2001). Catastrophic shifts in ecosystems. Nature 413, 591-596

Scheffer, M., Bascompte, J., Brock, W. A., Brovkin, V., Carpenter, S.R., Dakos, V., Held, H., Nes, E.H., Rietkerk, M. and Sugihara, G. (2009). Early-warning signals for critical transitions. Nature 461(3), 53-59

Schellnhuber, H.J. (2008). Global warming: Stop worrying, start panicking? Proceedings of the National Academy of Sciences 105(38), 14239-14240

Scherr, S.J. and McNeely, J.A. (eds.) (2008). Biodiversity Conservation and Agricultural Sustainability: Towards a New Paradigm of 'Ecoagriculture' Landscapes. Philosophical Transactions of the Royal Society 363(1491), 477-494

Schmidt, G.A. and Shindell, D.T. (2003). Atmospheric composition, radiative forcing, and climate change as a consequence of a massive methane release from gas hydrates. Paleoceanography 18(1), 1004

Schrope, M. (2009). When money grows on trees: Protecting forests offers a quick and cost-effective way of reducing emissions, but agreeing a means to do so won't be easy. Nature Reports Climate Change, 14 August 2009

Schubert, R., Schellnhuber, H.-J., Buchmann, N., Epiney, A., Grießhammer, R., Kulessa, M., Messner, D., Rahmstorf, S. and Schmid, J. (2006). The Future Oceans: warming up, rising high, turning sour. Special Report of the German Advisory Council on Global Change (WBGU)

Schuur, E.A.G., Bockheim, J., Canadell, J.G., Euskirchen, E., Field, C.B., Goryachkin, S.V., Hagemann, S., Kuhry, P., Lafleur, P.M., Lee, H., Mazhitova, G., Nelson, F.E., Rinke, A., Romanovsky, V.E., Shiklomanov, N., Tarnocai, C., Venevsky, S., Vorel, J.G. and Zimov, S.A. (2008). Vulnerability of Permafrost Carbon to Climate Change: Implications for the Global Carbon Cycle. BioScience 58(8), 701-714

Scott, M. (2008). Rapid Retreat Ice Shelf Loss Along Canada's Ellesmere Coast, Sept 8, 2008. Featured article http://earthobservatory.nasa.gov/Features/Ellesmere/

Seager, R., Ting, M., Held, I., Kushnir, Y., Lu, J., Vecchi, G., Huang, H-P., Harnik, N., Leetmaa, A., Lau, N., Li, C., Velez, J. and Naik, N. (2007). Model Projections of an Imminent Transition to a More Arid Climate in Southwestern North America. Science 316(5828), 1181-1184

Seastedt, T.R., Hobbs, R.J. and Suding, K.N. (2008). Management of novel ecosystems: are novel approaches required? Frontiers in Ecology and the Environment 6(10), 547-553

SEG (2007). Confronting Climate Change: Avoiding the Unmanageable and Managing the Unavoidable [Rosina M. Bierbaum, John P. Holdren, Michael C. MacCracken, Richard H. Moss, and Peter H. Raven (eds.)]. Scientific Expert Group on Climate Change. Report prepared for the United Nations Commission on Sustainable Development. Sigma Xi, Research Triangle Park, NC, and the United Nations Foundation, Washington, DC, 144 pp.

Seidel, D.J., Fu, Q., Randel, W.J. and Reichler, T.J. (2008). Widening of the tropical belt in a changing climate. Nature Geoscience 1, 21-24

Seinfeld, J. (2008). Black carbon and brown clouds. Nature Geoscience 1, 15-16

Serreze, M.C. and Francis, J.A. (2006). The Arctic amplification debate. Climate Change 76, 241-264

Serreze, M.C., Barrett, A.P., Slater, A.G., Woodgate, R.A., Aagaard, K., Lammers, R.B., Steele, M., Moritz, R., Meredith, M. and Lee, C.M. (2006). The large-scale fresh water cycle of the Arctic. Journal of Geophysical Research 111, C11010

Serreze, M.C., Holland, M.M. and Stroeve, J.C. (2007). Perspectives on the Arctic's shrinking sea-ice cover. Science 315, 1533-1536

Severinghaus, J.P. and Brook, E.J. (1999). Abrupt climate change at the end of the last glacial period inferred from trapped air in polar ice. Science 286, 930-934

Severinghaus, J.P., Sowers, T., Brook, E.J., Alley, R.B. and Bender, M.L. (1998). Timing of abrupt climate change at the end of the Younger Dryas interval from thermally fractionated gases in polar ice. Nature 391, 141-146

Severinghaus, J.P., Beaudette, R., Headly, M.A., Taylor, K. and Brook, E.J. (2009). Oxygen-18 of O_2 Records the Impact of Abrupt Climate Change on the Terrestrial Biosphere. Science 324, 1431-1434

Sheffer, G., Olsen, S.M. and Pederson, J.O.P. (2009). Long-term ocean oxygen depletion in response to carbon dioxide emissions from fossil fuels. Nature Geoscience 2, 105-109

Shindell, D.T. (2008). Cool Ozone. Nature Geoscience 1, 85-86

Shindell, D.T. and Faluvegi, G. (2009). Climate response to regional radiative forcing during the twentieth century. Nature Geoscience 2, 294-300

Shindell, D.T. and Schmidt, G.A. (2004). Southern Hemisphere climate response to ozone changes and greenhouse gas increases. Geophysical Research Letters 31, L18209

Siddall, M., Stocker, T.S., and Clark, P.U. (2009). Constraints on future sea-level rise from past sea-level change. Nature Geoscience (In Press) Published online: 26 July 2009

Silverman, J., Lazar, B., Cao. L., Caldeira, K. and Erez, J. (2009). Coral reefs may start dissolving when atmospheric CO_2 doubles. Geophysical Research Letters 36, L05606

Skovmand, B. (2007). The Svalbard International Seed Depository. The Nordic Genebank, Norway. www.ecpgr.cgiar.org/Steeringcommittee/SC10/InfnewDev/SISD.doc

Smith, J.B., Schneider, S.H., Oppenheimer, M., Yohe, G.W., Hare, W., Mastrandrea, M.D., Patwardhan, A., Burton, I., Corfee-Morlot, J., Magazda, C.H.D., Füssel, H.-M., Pittock, A.B., Rahman, A., Suarez, A. and van Ypersele, J.-P. (2009). Assessing dangerous climate change through an update of the Intergovernmental Panel on Climate Change (IPCC) "reasons for concern". Proceedings of the National Academy of Sciences 106, 4133–4137

Sole, A., Payne, T., Bamber, J., Nienow, P. and Krabill, W. (2008). Testing hypotheses of the cause of peripheral thinning of the Greenland Ice Sheet: is land-terminating ice thinning at anomalously high rates? The Cryosphere 2, 673-710

Solomina, O., Haeberli, W., Kull, C. and Wiles, G. (2008). Historical and Holocene glacier-climate relations: general concepts and overview. Global and Planetary Change 60, 1-9

Solomon, S., Plattner, G.-K., Knutti, R. and Friedlingstein, P. (2009). Irreversible climate change due to carbon dioxide emissions. Proceedings of the National Academy of Sciences 106(6), 1704-1709

Solomon, S., Qin, D., Manning, M. Chen, Z., Marquis, M., Avery, K.B., Tignor, M., and Miller, H.L. (2007). IPCC, Climate Change 2007: The Physical Science Basis. Contribution of Working Group I to the Fourth Assessment Report of the Intergovernmental Panel on Climate Change, Cambridge University Press, Cambridge, United Kingdom and New York, NY, USA, 2007

Son, S.-W., Polvani, L.M., Waugh, D.W., Akiyoshi, H., Garcia, R., Kinnison, D., Pawson, S., Rozanov, E., Shepherd, T.G. and Shibata, K. (2008). The Impact of Stratospheric Ozone Recovery on the Southern Hemisphere Westerly Jet. Science 320(5882), 1486-1489

Steig, E., Schneider, P., Rutherford, S.D., Mann, M.E., Comiso, J.C. and Shindell, D.T. (2009). Warming of the Antarctic ice-sheet surface since the 1957 International Geophysical Year. Nature 457, 459-463

Steinacher, M., Joos, F., Frölicher, T. L., Plattner, G.-K. and Doney, S.C. (2009). Imminent ocean acidification in the Arctic projected with the NCAR global coupled carbon cycle-climate model. Biogeosciences 6, 515–533

Strassburg, B., Turner, R.K., Fisher, B., Schaeffer, R. and Lovett, A. (2009). Reducing emissions from deforestation – The "combined incentives" mechanism and empirical simulations. Global Environmental Change 19, 265-278

Stroeve, J., Holland, M.M., Meier, W., Scambos, T. and Serreze, M. (2007). Arctic sea ice decline: Faster than forecast. Geophysical Research Letters 34, L09501

Stroeve, J., Serreze, M., Drobot, S., Gearheard, S., Holland, M., Maslanik, J., Meier, W. and Scambos, T. (2008). Arctic sea ice extent plummets in 2007. EOS, Transactions, American Geophysical Union 89(2), 13

Surowiecki, J. (2008). The Perils of Efficiency. The New Yorker 84(38), 46

Swaminathan, M.S. (2009). Gene Banks for a Warming Planet. Science 325(5940), 517

Swanson, K.L. and Tsonis, A.A. (2009). Has the climate recently shifted? Geophysical Research Letters 36, L06711

Tarnocai, C., Canadell, J.G., Schuur, E.A.G., Kuhry, P., Mazhitova, G. and Zimov, S. (2009). Soil organic carbon pools in the northern circumpolar permafrost region. *Global Biogeochemical Cycles* 23, GB2023

Tedesco, M., Abdalati, W. and Zwally, J. (2007). Persistent surface snowmelt over Antarctica (1987-2006) from 19.35 GHz brightness temperatures. *Geophysical Research Letters* 34, L18504

Tewksbury, J.J., Huey, R.B. and Deutsch, C.A. (2008). Putting the Heat on Tropical Animals. *Science* 320(5881), 1296-1297

Thampanya, U., Vermaat, J.E., Sinsakul, S. and Panapitukkul, N. (2006). Coastal erosion and mangrove progradation of Southern Thailand. *Estuarine, Coastal and Shelf Science* 82(1-2), 75-85

Thompson, D.W.J. and Solomon, S. (2002). Interpretation of recent Southern Hemisphere climate change. *Science* 296, 895-899

Tilmes, S., Müller, R. and Salawitch, R. (2008). The Sensitivity of Polar Ozone Depletion to Proposed Geoengineering Schemes. *Science* 320, 1201-1204

Toggweiler, J.R. (2009). Shifting westerlies. *Science* 323(5920), 1434-1435

Toggweiler, J.R. and Russell, J. (2008). Ocean circulation in a warming climate. *Nature* 451(7176), 286-288

Trenberth, K.E. (2001). Earth System Processes, Encyclopedia of Global Environmental Change, T. Munn (Ed. in Chief), Vol. 1. The Earth System: Physical and Chemical Dimensions of Global Environmental Change, M.C. MacCracken and J. S. Perry (Eds), John Wiley & Sons Ltd., 13–30

Trenberth, K.E. and Dai, A. (2007). Effects of Mount Pinatubo volcanic eruption on the hydrological cycle as an analog of geoengineering. *Geophysical Research Letters* 34, L15702

Trumper, K., Bertzky, M., Dickson, B., van der Heijden, G., Jenkins, M., Manning, P. June (2009). The Natural Fix? The role of ecosystems in climate mitigation. A UNEP rapid response assessment. UNEP-WCMC, Cambridge, UK

Turner, J., Comiso, J.C., Marshall, G.J., Lachlan-Cope, T.A., Bracegirdle, T., Maksym, T., Meredith, M.P., Wang, Z. and Orr, A. (2009). Non-annular atmospheric circulation change induced by stratospheric zone depletion and its role in the recent increase of Antarctic sea ice extent. *Geophysical Research Letters* 36, L08502

UCSD (2009). ARGO: Part of the Integrated Global Observation Strategy. http://www.argo.ucsd.edu/About_Argo.html [Accessed 14 September 2009]

UN (2008). Sustainable Development Report on Africa: Five-Year Review of the Implementation of the World Summit on Sustainable Development Outcomes in Africa. United Nations Economic Commission for Africa, Addis Ababa, Ethiopia, April 2008

UNEP (2007). Global Environment Outlook 4: Environment for Development. United Nations Environment Programme, Nairobi

UNEP (2008a). From conflict to peacebuilding: The role of natural resources and the environment. UNEP Expert Advisory Group on Environment, Conflict and Peacebuilding

UNEP (2008b). Assessment of the State of the Marine Environment. United Nations Environment Programme, Division of Early Warning and Assessment. http://www.unep.org/dewa/assessments/Ecosystems/water/marineassessment/index.as

UNEP (2008c). UNEP Year Book: An Overview of Our Changing Environment. United Nations Environment Programme, Nairobi

UNEP (2009). UNEP Year Book: New Science and Developments in our Changing Environment. United Nations Environment Programme, Nairobi

UNEP/GRID-Arendal (2002). The Greenhouse Effect. Vital climate graphics, United Nations Environment Programme, http://www.grida.no/climate/vital/index.htm

UNEP/GRID-Arendal (1998). (eds.) Rekacewicz, P., Desforges, M. Map production. BARENTS watch 1998. An environmental atlas. UNEP/GRID-Arendal, Svanhovd Environmental Centre, the Directorate for Nature Management and the Norwegian Polar Institute

UNEP-WCMC (2006). In the Front Line: Shoreline Protection and Other Ecosystem Services from Mangroves and Coral Reefs. UNEP-WCMC, Cambridge

University of Maryland (2009). http://www.bbc.co.uk/blogs/climatechange/2009/04/ [Accessed 14 August 2009]

Våge, K., Pickart, R.S., Thierry, V., Reverdin, G., Lee, C.M., Petrie, B., Agnew, T.A., Wong, A. and Ribergaard, M.H. (2009). Surprising return of deep convection to the subpolar North Atlantic Ocean in winter 2007–2008. *Nature Geoscience* 2, 76-72

Vaughan, N.E., Lenton, T.M., Shepherd, J.G. (2009). Climate change mitigation: tradeoffs between delay and strength of action required. *Climatic Change*, 1-15 (In Press)

Vermaat, J.E. and Thampanya, U. (2007). Mangroves mitigate tsunami damage: A further response. *Estuarine, Coastal and Shelf Science* 75, 564

Victor, D.G., Morgan, M.G., Apt, J., Steinbruner, J. and Ricke, K. (2009). The Geoengineering Option – A Last Resort Against Global Warming? *Foreign Affairs* 88(2), 64-76

Voss, M. and Montoya, J.P. (2009). Nitrogen cycles: Oceans apart. *Nature* 461, 49-50

Walter, K.M., Smith, L.C. and Chapin III, F.S. (2007). Methane bubbling from northern lakes: present and future contributions to the global methane budget. *Philosophical Transactions of the Royal Society A* 365(1856), 1657-1676

Wang, M. and Overland, J.E. (2009). A sea ice free summer Arctic within 30 years? *Geophysical Research Letters* 36, L07502

Wang, M., Overland, J.E., Kattsov, V., Walsh, J.E, Zhang, X. and Pavlova, T. (2007). Intrinsic versus forced variation in coupled climate model simulations over the Arctic during the 20th century. *Journal of Climate* 20(6), 1093–1107.

Ward, B.B., Devol, A.H., Rich, J.J., Chang, B.X., Bulow, S.E., Naik, H., Pratihary, A. and Jayakumar, A. (2009). Denitrification as the dominant nitrogen loss process in the Arabian Sea. *Nature* 461, 78-81

Weaver, A.J., Clark, P.U., Brook, E., Cook, E.R., Delworth, T.L. and Steffen, K. (2008). Abrupt Climate Change – A Report by the US Climate Change Science Program. U.S. Geological Survey, Reston, VA, 459

Westbrook, G.K., Thatcher, K.E., Rohling, E.J., Piotrowski, A.M., Pälike, H., Osborne, A.H., Nisbet, E.G., Minshull, T.A., Lanoisellé, M., James, R.H., Huhnerbach, V., Green, D., Fisher, R.E., Crocker, A.J., Chabert, A., Bolton, C., Beszczynska-Möller, A., Berndt, C. and Aquilina, A. (2009). Escape of methane gas from the seabed along the West Spitsbergen continental margin. *Geophysical Research Letters* 36, L15608

WGMS (2008a). Global glacier changes: facts and figures. UNEP/World Glacier Monitoring Service, Zurich

WGMS (2008b). Glacier mass balance data 2005-2006. UNEP/World Glacier Monitoring Service, Zurich

Williams, J.W., Jackson, S.T. and Kutzbach, J.E. (2007). Projected distributions of novel and disappearing climates by 2100 AD. *Proceedings of the National Academy of Sciences* 104(14), 5738-5742

Winton, M. (2006). Amplified Arctic climate change: What does surface albedo feedback have to do with it? *Geophysical Research Letters* 33, L23504

WMO (2009). Progress Report on the Implementation of the Global Observing System for Climate in Support of the UNFCCC 2004-2008. August 2009, GCOS-129 World Meteorological Station-TD/No. 1489, GOOS-173, GTOS-70

Wood, H.L., Spicer, J.I., and Widdicombe, S. (2008). Ocean acidification may increase calcification rates, but at a cost. *Proceedings of the Royal Society* 275, 1767–73

Wootton, J.T., Pfister, C.A., and Forester, J.D. (2009). Dynamic patterns and ecological impacts of declining ocean pH in a high-resolution multi-year dataset. *Proceedings of the National Academy of Sciences* (In Press)

WWF (2005). Marine Protected Areas, Providing a future for fish and people. World Wild Fund for Nature

Yashayaev, I. and Loder, J.W. (2009). Enhanced production of Labrador Sea Water in 2008. *Geophysical Research Letters* 36, L01606

Yool, A., Shepherd, J.G., Bryden, H.L. and Oschlies, A. (2009). Low efficiency of nutrient translocation for enhancing oceanic uptake of carbon dioxide *Journal of Geophysical Research* 114, C08009

Zachos, J.C., Lohmann, K.C., Walker, J.C.G. and Wise, S.W. (1993). Abrupt Climate Change and Transient Climates During the Paleogene: A Marine Perspective. *Journal of Geology* 100, 191-213

Zemp, M., Hoelzle, M. and Haeberli, W. (2009). Six decades of glacier mass balance observations – a review of the worldwide monitoring network. *Annals of Glaciology* 50, 101–111

Zimov, S.A., Schuur, E.A.G. and Chapin III., F.S. (2006). Climate change: Permafrost and the global carbon budget. *Science* 312(5780), 1612-1613

Zwally, H.J., Comiso, J.C., Parkinson, C.L., Cavalieri, D.J. and Gloersen, P. (2002). Variability of Antarctic sea ice 1979-1998. *Journal of Geophysical Research* 107(C5), 3041

Acknowledgements

This Compendium is a product of the strong dedication of several individuals, whose knowledge, expertise, and insight helped produce what proved to be a very challenging endeavour. We are indebted to a number of people in particular, for their extraordinary investment in and support of the effort, including Michael MacCracken, W. Tad Pfeffer, Robert W. Corell, Wilfried Haeberli, Ghassam Asrar, Valerie Percival, and Timothy M. Lenton.

We would also like to acknowledge the tremendous support and patience of our collaborating partners and colleagues at the Scientific Committee on Problems of the Environment, the World Climate Research Programme, and the World Meteorological Organization.

Scientific Committee on Problems of the Environment (SCOPE)

World Meteorological Organization

Production Team:

Márton Bálint

Jason Jabbour

Catherine McMullen

Alex Horton

Support Team:

Sylvia Adams

Susanne Bech

Marcella Carew

Susan Greenwood Etienne

Brian Harding

Katalin Hegedüs

Anna Kontorov

Nicolas Kraff

Ludovic Machaira

Nick Nuttall

Véronique Plocq Fichelet

Kaveh Zahedi